Miracles in Lady Lane

The Ipswich Shrine at the Westgate

G. Fint

Miracles in Lady Lane

The Ipswich Shrine at the Westgate

by John Blatchly and Diarmaid MacCulloch

2013

Published by:
J. M. Blatchly
2013

Text copyright © J. M. Blatchly and D. MacCulloch

ISBN 978-0-9564584-2-1

Text set in Book Antiqua
Design & layout: M. N. Sanford

Printed and bound in the United Kingdom by:
Henry Ling Limited
The Dorset Press
Dorchester
Dorset
DT1 1HD

Contents

Preface	1
Introduction	2
The shrine's prehistory and location	2
'An image underground': the cult begins	9
A new rector: Dr John Bailey	14
Wonders and miracles: the Maid of Ipswich	20
The Maid's first name: Jane or Anne?	27
A witness to the wonders: St Matthews's font	30
Two clerics clash: Wolsey and Bailey	38
The coming of Reformation: destruction	46
Aftermath: myths and survivals	58
Appendix: Sir Robert Curson's narrative	69
Notes	75
Index nominum	90

Preface

LADY LANE is today truncated and somewhat barren, passing between two shops built in the 1960s of dark engineering brick. Shaded by three ornamental trees, there is a small bronze sculpture, shown here. We have attempted to bring this almost lost street back to life, from the medieval days when it was part of an ancient Ipswich suburb as 'the road to Mandulve's Well', to its long possession of its present name. Much has happened here in church and churchyard, chapels of two dedications and first the Hospital of St John and then, Edmund Daundy's fifteen almshouses built and endowed for the poor of the extramural parish of St Matthew's. A king and a queen, a cardinal and a mitred abbot came to Lady Lane, all in the space of a decade in Tudor times, as did generations of pilgrim crowds to the Shrine which flourished here until the Reformation swept both image and building away.

This project has grown from the length of a potential newspaper single-spread to a substantial book, partly through our own indiscretion, but also thanks to the help provided by many friends. We are especially grateful for the assistance of Anthony Breen, David Dymond, Charles Farrow, Christopher Fletcher-Vane, Chris Given-Wilson, the late Peter Northeast, Steven Plunkett, Nigel Saul and Roger and Stella Wolfe. Simon Knott has supplied us with his superb photographs of the font in St Matthew's Church. We owe a great deal to Martin Sanford who has not only designed the book and put it through the press, but in his amazingly agile way with the web trawled up interesting images and other references to the subject which we might otherwise have missed.

JOHN BLATCHLY
DIARMAID MacCULLOCH
2013

Madonna and Child in
Lady Lane
by Robert Mellamphy

Introduction

This is a study of one of late medieval England's most celebrated shrines, home to an image of the Blessed Virgin Mary, destroyed by Henry VIII in 1538: the Chapel of Our Lady of Grace. Until now, it has been thought that Ipswich had not preserved any visible original relic of this shrine; its foundations lie buried in an unpromising setting beside the town's inner ring road, now marked by a bronze image of the Virgin and Child by the sculptor Robert Mellamphy, placed there in 1990, while in the Anglican parish church of St Mary Elms, a new shrine has arisen to replace it [1]. In the course of the story we present here, reconstructing the shrine's origin, flourishing and destruction, we suggest to the reader that there is much more to discover: ancient local witnesses survive. There is a beautiful, unspoilt and hitherto unrecognised monument to the most celebrated events in the shrine's history: it is the font in the parish church of St Matthew, a matter of a few-score yards from the site of the Chapel of Our Lady. We further suggest that the now-redundant parish church of St Nicholas nearby incorporates reused elements of the shrine chapel itself.

The Elizabethan Protestant historian John Foxe gleefully related the end of the shrine of Our Lady of Grace in 1538, making it clear that its destruction formed part of a concerted nationwide campaign by Thomas Cromwell in the name of King Henry VIII:

> You heard before by the kynges Iniunctions aboue expressed, and directed out an[no] 1538. how all such Images & pictures, which were abused with Pilgrimage or offrings or any Idolatrie, where abolished: by vertue of which Iniunction, diuers Idols & especially the most notable stockes of Idolatrie, were taken downe the same yeare. 1538. as the Images of Walsingham, Ipswich, Worcester, the Ladye of Wilsdon [Willesden], Thomas Becket, with many moe, hauing engings [engines] to make their eyes to open and role about, and other partes of their body to styrre, and many other false iugglynges, as the bloud of Hayles, and such lyke, wherwith the simple people a long tyme had bene deceiued. All which were espyed out, and destroyed. [2]

We will discover that this dramatic finale was matched by an equally dramatic beginning.

The shrine's prehistory and location

The creation of Our Lady's shrine (to which, for convenience, we will generally refer as Gracechurch) is an example of a general tendency in northern European devotion from the eleventh century onwards to develop cults around statues of Our Lady, rather than around the tomb of some locally-celebrated individual. The great attraction of such cults was that they could start anywhere, without the

The sites marked A to G on the outline map of part of the parish of St Matthew's have property boundaries which appeared to survive from the 14th century through to 1674 when John Ogilby sent Gregory King and Robert Felgate to survey Ipswich for a nine sheet plan of the town at a scale of 100 feet to the inch. They have been cleared of all buildings here, except that the seven Daundy almshouses on the west side of Lady Lane are shown as a vertical strip invading B. They faced the eight eastern almshouses across the Lane.

A was from the early 12th century the site of All Saints Church and its yard, which it retained when it became All Saints Chapel dependent on St Matthew's. From about 1400 the name changed to Our Lady's Chapel, popularly Gracechurch.

B *without the seven almshouses of Daundy's foundation before 1515 as explained above.* In three extents dating from 1334 and 1343 this was referred to as the almshouse for the poor and St John's Hospital and its pightle. No earlier or later mentions have been found. In 1409 the site passed from Rideout to Ady, indication surely that St John's Hospital had closed.

C and D were held by Halteby, late Mundy in 1334 and 1338, but in 1342-43 C was either Halteby's or Laweman's, and D belonged to Elias Laweman.

E and F were in 1334 and 1338 late de Westhale, but in 1342/43 E was Halteby's or Laweman's and F was Laweman's.

G was the Hospital enclosure from 1334 and 1338, but in 1342/43 Harney's Kroft, and in 1409 described as late Laweman's.

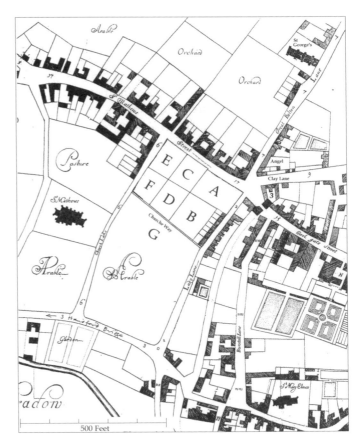

Excerpt from Ogilby's map of Ipswich 1674.

need for any physical relics of a body: essential in the case of Our Lady. With the alleged exception of some items of clothing and a certain amount of milk, she had not left any bodily relics behind, thanks to her Assumption into Heaven. Hence in their inevitable absence, all a local church needed was to invest in a statue, which with luck, divine favour, local enthusiasm or assiduous salesmanship, might produce evidence of its miraculous power and become the focus of pilgrimage.

Gracechurch was situated immediately outside the defensive precinct of the town to the west, confronting the West Gate or Bargate, on the main road across Suffolk out of town towards Bury St Edmunds. By the seventeenth century, when John Ogilby, Cosmographer Royal, had Ipswich surveyed in 1674 for his astonishingly accurate and informative large-scale map of the borough, the relevant section of this main road west just outside the town gate had acquired its modern name, St Matthew's Street, and for convenience, this is how we will refer to it in the present study. A north-south lane skirted the outer edge of the western town defences, crossing St Matthew's Street, and the section of that lane south of St Matthew's Street came to be known as Lady Lane; indeed this is still its name. Gracechurch was on the south-west corner of the road-intersection of St Matthew's Street and Lady Lane, immediately to the north of a paired row of almshouses founded by Edmund Daundy in the early sixteenth century. The Daundy almshouses continued to flank Lady Lane up to their demolition in the late nineteenth century.

From an early date there are references to a number of religious buildings in this extra-mural area around St Matthew's Street. There was a parish church of St George, a building mentioned in Domesday Book, situated to the north of St Matthew's Street west of the north-south lane; its structure survived up to the early nineteenth century, and it may have had the only round tower in any Ipswich parish church. Besides this, there was a Hospital of St John and a nearby church (later called a chapel) of All Saints.[3] As will become apparent below (pp. 59-60), we can be certain that although All Saints did not appear in Domesday, it had elaborate sculptural decoration of the early Norman period. It is also clear by comparing topographical descriptions given in documents of various periods that at the turn of the fourteenth and fifteenth centuries, All Saints became known as the shrine of our Lady of Grace, having housed a Marian cultic image since the early fourteenth century.

A couple of centuries before that transformation, All Saints' chapel came to be included in an extra-mural parish of St Matthew to the west of the town. St

St George's Church probably from the east. The window appears to lack its original Y-tracery. Lithograph of 1820 by George Rowe, aged 16.

Matthew's, a once-generously endowed parish which has retained its status as a rectory rather than a vicarage to the present day, was seemingly created in the late twelfth or early thirteenth century, as the first mention of the parish, its priest and appended chapel of All Saints occurs in royal exchequer records in 1219, already in the patronage of the Crown.[4] St Matthew is an unusual dedication in England, and that fact alone would indicate that it predated any presence of a wonder-working image of Our Lady, whose name would surely have taken precedence in a new foundation.[5] The association between parish church and shrine was nevertheless eventually to prove of great significance. It is worth noting that over time, the name of the chapel of Our Lady appears to have supplanted the mention of All Saints in connection with St Matthew, and All Saints only survived as a ghostly presence in the most formal of documents about ecclesiastical taxation.[6] Our starting-point in tracing that process is a pair of bequests in 1315 to both All Saints' chapel and St Matthew's church, by a widow with the unusual name of Sayeena (Sabina or Selina?) Leew; might her husband have been a migrant from Europe? She left rents from various of her tenements in the town to pay for seven tapers before the altar of St Katherine the Virgin in the chapel of All Saints and three lamps burning in the chapel

5

while masses were celebrated, as well as two lamps in St Matthew's before the Rood and the altar of St Mary the Virgin.[7]

There are other bequests recorded in the Ipswich Court of Petty Recognisances during the fourteenth century which help us to fix the position of this All Saints' church or chapel. They reveal that it was directly beside the hospital or almshouses dedicated to St John. The first of these, at the Borough Court held on 9 December 1334 (Friday after the Conception of the Blessed Virgin Mary, 8 Edward III), records a land transaction by John Haltebe, or de Halteby, one of the most powerful men in the town at that time, though by no means one of the most popular. Halteby exhibited a charter from John, son of Thomas de Weston and his wife Joan, granting him among other property a tenement late of John Mundy 'next to the gate of Ipswich called the New Gaol' (*juxta illas portas Gippiwici que vocantur le Newegahole*), together with shops nearby this tenement in the parish of St Matthew's Ipswich, lying between the Hospital of St John on the east, and on the west, tenements which were Walter de Westhale's.[8]

More details about these same shops appear in a further record of Halteby's ownership in the court held four years later, on 27 February 1338 (Friday after St Matthias, 12 Edward III). Here the property is described as a tenement granted to Halteby by John de Westone in the parish of St Matthew between on the east, the hospital of the poor beside the chapel of All Saints (*inter hospitalem pauperum iuxta capellam Omnium Sanctorum*) and on the west, the tenement formerly of Walter de Westhale. Its north head was on the highway, and the south head was on the enclosure belonging to the said hospital.[9]

These two records provide a useful picture of three burgage tenements (the central tenement or three shops being Halteby's property), their long axes north-south, with the highway (St Matthew's Street) to their north. The easternmost is the Hospital of St John immediately beside All Saints' Church, and we learn that besides lying alongside Halteby's tenement, the hospital had a field bordering its south side. The whole block of three is very close and to the west of the New Gaol, which incorporated the West Gate of the borough. So it is fairly certain even from these two grants that the three tenements can be identified with the properties depicted on Ogilby's much later map which include, at the east, the site of what would in the fifteenth and sixteenth centuries become the shrine church, Lady Lane and the Daundy almshouses. Just to confirm the position of this block of properties on St Matthew's Street, we need to consider a slightly later grant, from the borough recognisances of 15/16

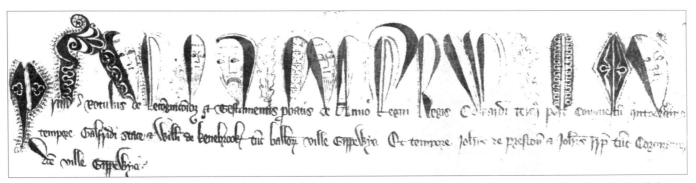

Initials from the head of Recognisance Roll C/2/4/1/30 (1342), which makes mention of the road to Mandulve's Well, later, Lady Lane. The clerk recording the Court proceedings often headed the roll with uncials with large risers and occasionally filled the loops with caricatured faces. Reproduced courtesy of SRO Ipswich and Ipswich Borough Council.

Edward III (1342-43). In these, John le Kurch of Ipswich exhibited a charter from Benedict, son of Peter le Jay and his wife Joan, granting him land called Harneys Kroft in the parish of St Matthew. On its north side was the curtilage of Elias Laweman and a pightle called 'le Almesehous'; to its east was the highway from the church of All Saints by the walls of Ipswich as far as 'Mandulveswelle' (Mandulve's Well). On its west was the east part of the churchyard of St Matthew, and its remaining head (to the south) was on the highway from Horsewade Mill towards Shirehouse Hill. To judge from this description, the enclosure owned by the hospital to the south of the

land owned by Halteby in 1338 can probably be identified with this 'Harneys Kroft' in 1342.[10]

The siting of All Saints' is now conclusively demonstrated. It can only have lain in the easternmost of the three burgage plots to the south of St Matthew's Street, bounded to the east by what was to become Lady Lane ('the highway from All Saints to Mandulveswelle along the borough walls') and to the west by a minor road which bounds the east side of St Matthew's churchyard (but which in the twenty-first century has become a monstrous through-highway). Beside All Saints was 'le Almesehous', otherwise known as the Hospital of St John. A little distance

7

away to the south was a major and ancient east-west road from Horsewade Mill, a mill on the river Gipping as it ran into the town: this is the road which still exists as Handford Road (and is marked by '3' on Ogilby's map). What also needs to be emphasised is that these locations of All Saints and the St John's are also the later sites of the shrine chapel of Our Lady, Gracechurch and of Daundy's almshouses. Evidently both chapel and hospital changed their identity in the medieval period, and the next task is to fix the approximate dates and the reasons for these shifts.

The last mention of All Saints in connection with the incumbency of St Matthew's church was in 1406, at the Crown's institution to St Matthew's of William Kyrkeham. In 1407, on the next presentation to the living by Henry IV, it was called '*the chapel annexed to the same*'.[11] Its churchyard is mentioned for the last time only slightly later. On 10 December 1409 (the Tuesday before the Feast of St Lucy, 11 Henry IV), the Ipswich Petty Court of Recognisances records a transaction in which John Rideout of Ipswich and his wife Alice granted to William Ady and William Rideout of Ipswich a tenement and curtilage with its north head on the churchyard of All Saints' Chapel and on the east the highway, with to the south lands formerly of Elias Laweman. As we have seen, Laweman's curtilage had been mentioned in the grant

of 1342, but the bounds described in the present grant suggest that Laweman's curtilage of 1342 was not the same as the former Laweman property mentioned here (indeed, this Laweman property may well be the same as John le Kurch's Harness Kroft).[12]

The tenement and curtilage being conveyed in the grant of 1409 is significant in itself. The bounds place it on the site which would a century later be occupied by the western block of Edmund Daundy's almshouses, and which was also previously the site of the Hospital of St John. Perhaps Ady and the Rideouts were trustees making a regrant of Hospital property for legal reasons, but if so, it seems strange that the Hospital itself was not named. Maybe there was some evasion going on, perhaps to avoid mortmain legislation; yet there is no doubt of the Hospital's continued existence: it struggled on in a very reduced form through the fifteenth century. At the Lete Courts for the East Ward on 5 June 1487 and 27 May 1488, lists of people were presented to be fined as 'gannokers', that is, ale brewers on a domestic scale, who were allowed to continue brewing if they paid a fine or fee each year. All are named except the last person on both lists, who is simply described as 'the Woman at the almshous'. Either she was so anonymous and unimportant that it was not worth recording her name, or this permission was a recognized perquisite of whoever the inhabitant of the almshouse happened to be: she was formally allowed to make a small profit above her fine, as part of her meagre subsistence (and maybe there was something of a rapid turn-over among these elderly ladies).

So St John's Hospital was still in existence, at least a century and a half after its foundation beside All Saints', but it was a sadly reduced survival of whatever ambitions had created it. Then suddenly in the will of the great Ipswich benefactor Edmund Daundy proved in 1515, there appear Daundy's almshouses, which are not identified as dedicated to St John, and are on a much grander scale. We will return to their significance in the later history and development of the shrine; but first, we must investigate how the cult of Our Lady originated in the chapel of All Saints in the early fourteenth century.

'An image underground': the cult begins

We have established the identity of All Saints with the later shrine, and it is very fortunate that we can pin down the origin of the cult quite precisely, thanks to a small piece of bureaucracy which carried the story of its beginnings all the way to the Holy Father in the papal palace at Avignon. On 29th March (4th of the Kalends of April) 1327, a papal clerk in Avignon, not without puzzlement as to how to pronounce a Suffolk place-name which has always given foreigners trouble, penned a commission and mandate to the Bishop of Norwich to relax sixty days of enjoined penance to penitents who would contribute to the completion of the chapel in the place called 'Ypeçug' in his diocese. Here a representation of the Blessed Virgin had been found underground, and several great miracles had taken place.[13]

This is actually one of the earliest of such papal grants of indulgences to Marian shrines in Europe. From the narrative details, we may deduce that the discovery was fairly recent, and allowing time for the miracles, we can hazard that it had taken place in 1325 or 1326. What an extraordinary story this is! Yet there is no reason to doubt its truth. It is noticeable that this Marian shrine was not located in any of the four parish churches dedicated to Our Lady which the town possessed by the Norman period: St Mary Elms, St Mary Quay, St Mary Stoke and St Mary-le-Tower. Instead, it was placed in a relatively humble and subsidiary extra-mural chapel, which by the sound of the papal mandate to its potential devotees, was in need of drastic repair. It may have been that the image of Our Lady was discovered in the course of beginning that repair-work, and perhaps the repairs were inspired by the founding of St John's Hospital next door.

Thus this was not a case of a church of St Mary steadily promoting an image of its patron saint; rather it was the accidental discovery of a buried statue, and that must have added to the sense that it possessed a miraculous quality. Those who in the sixteenth century destroyed Our Lady of Ipswich's image on a bonfire (not to mention an Essex Lollard who a decade before had hated it and wanted to burn it) reveal to us that it was carved of wood: another reason for marvel, no doubt, as it emerged from the ground or the foundations of All Saints. The Romanesque church building in which it was found possessed quite exceptional carved stone decoration in a style which would have been quite alien to fourteenth-century viewers, and if the wooden image was from the same much earlier period, one can see why it would have so impressed people with its strangeness. From such excitement, it was not difficult for miracles to follow, as was to prove the case once more two centuries later, as we will discover. And it was presumably the exceptional circumstances which gave rise to the highly unusual designation of this particular manifestation of God's Mother as 'Our Lady of Grace', the description by which the Ipswich cult was invariably known over the next two centuries. Quite apart from the Annunciation salutation of the Angel Gabriel to the Mother of God which every medieval Christian knew, 'Hail Mary, full of grace', the discovery of the statue underground was evidently seen an act of peculiar divine favour or grace.

Now the cult was launched, and its spectacular beginning ensured the attention of the most powerful in the land. Edward III was known as a lavish patron of traditional cults with a particular devotion to Our Lady, and this is borne out by his account-books: he travelled or gave offerings to Marian shrines both at home and abroad, way beyond the tally of the most popular centres. In 1342 he sent a money gift to the Ipswich shrine, 'out of the King's particular devotion'.[14] The first known visit to the shrine by a member of the royal family in person came in 1402, from a young member of the newly-established Lancastrian dynasty. Henry IV's ten year-old daughter Princess Blanche of Lancaster spent nearly two months in Ipswich before her significant dynastic marriage to Prince Louis the future Elector Palatine. The first public engagement arranged for her on her arrival on 30 April 1402 after a few days in Colchester was mass 'before a certain precious image in a chapel outside the town walls of Ipswich'. It received the offering of a quarter-mark which was standard throughout her subsequent public appearances at services at the Ipswich Whitefriars and Christ Church (Holy Trinity) Priory.[15] This might be seen as hardly more than a gesture of politeness to the nearest local shrine on the part of a monarch who was never very generous to the Church, but it is interesting that Gracechurch should have been chosen as the dramatic setting for the Princess's solemn entrance to the borough.

What is also significant is that the clerk compiling Princess Blanche's accounts did not give a dedication name to the chapel containing the 'precious image'; he was normally meticulous in such matters. As we have seen, he was writing in a decade of transition for the shrine: by the beginning of the fifteenth century, the original dedication of All Saints' Church was coming to be considered subsidiary to its cult of Our Lady which had blossomed during the fourteenth century. The chapel was renamed in popular perception, and perhaps then formally rededicated, for Our Lady. The date around 1400 would be consistent with the profile of East Anglia's other great Marian shrine at Walsingham, which despite its origin-story set in the eleventh century, only really gathered momentum as a goal for pilgrimage in the fourteenth and fifteenth centuries. Walsingham admittedly does seem to have taken its origin as a cult before the dramatic fourteenth-century discovery in Ipswich. In the 1530s, Bishop Hugh Latimer (a hostile observer) referred to the image of Our Lady in his own cathedral church of

Worcester alongside 'here old syster of Walsyngham, hyr younge syster of Ipswych', and that may have been a common perception of the relationship between the two: Walsingham was the older of the two shrines, and by comparison Ipswich was recent and junior.[16]

The impression of a deliberate and far-ranging reorganisation of St Matthew's parish life in the fifteenth century is reinforced by the fact that the dedications of altars were swapped between parish church and chapel. Whereas in 1315 Sayeena Leew had been able to make bequests to an altar of St Katherine at All Saints and an altar of Our Lady at St Matthew, by 1479 a parish testator asked for burial before the altar of St Katherine in St Matthew's church, with a chaplain to sing mass there for him. By that date or later, there is no further mention of an altar of Our Lady at St Matthew's.[17] Evidently, the two female saints had come to an arrangement over the previous century: St Katherine should not be in competition with Our Lady at the shrine church, and there was no point in having a second altar of Our Lady in the parish church.

By mid-century we have conclusive evidence that the parishioners of St Matthew's now regarded the former church of All Saints as the Chapel of Our Lady. When Walter Velwet of Ipswich made his will on 12

March 1458, he made a bequest of 3s 4d (quarter of a mark) to the fabric of a bridge between the chapel of the Blessed Virgin Mary of the same town and the gates of the King's prison (what a century before had been known as the 'New Gaol'), together with any other building needed there. Velwet also asked for burial in St Matthew's churchyard, and he left money to John Baker, a priest of the parish.[18] The scheme for repair of the bridge indicates that the town ditch was still a reality in the mid-fifteenth century. The project was evidently regarded as a family commitment, for the will of Thomas Welwette, chaplain, and evidently a relative, made only three years after that of Walter (1 March 1461), makes another quarter-mark bequest to the emendation of a bridge 'between the chapel of Blessed Mary and the gaol of the Lord King of the said town'.[19]

With no rival cults of significance in the town, Our Lady of Grace was clearly prospering during the fifteenth century. The household accounts of Sir John Howard, soon to become first Howard Duke of Norfolk, have an entry for 1481 recording that 'my Lord spent the vth day of May to Eppeswich to our Lady of Gras xs'.[20] This ten shillings was more generous than any previous individual donation we have noted, and reflects the fact that Sir John was intimately entangled with the affairs of Ipswich. His

chief seat was Tendryng Hall, not far away in the Stour Valley at Stoke-by-Nayland, and in the 1460s, the evidence is strong that he sent his son Thomas (later the second Howard duke of Norfolk) to board at the borough school.[21] It is not surprising that a Marian shrine also had a particular attraction for women: gentlewomen followed where a royal princess had led the way. So Margery Paston wrote to her husband John in the early 1480s, catching him up with family affairs in East Anglia: 'My Lady [Elizabeth] Caltrop [Calthorpe] hath ben at Geppeswiche on pylgry mache'.[22]

Exactly a century after Princess Blanche had made her offering, in February and March 1502, Henry VII's queen Elizabeth of York sent off her chaplain William Barton and Richard Milner of Binfield (apparently a layman) on two separate month-long tours of England to every Marian shrine that the Court could think of, with a few others thrown in as well. The context is clear: her teenage elder son Arthur, Prince of Wales, was now sinking into the illness which ended his life on 2 April 1502. In the vain quest to save the royal heir, Barton set off from the shrines at Windsor Castle via Our Lady of Eton up the Thames valley and into the Severn basin, then back through the Midlands (including Worcester Cathedral with its Our Lady, soon to be the site of the Prince's burial) to the battery of Our Ladies in East Anglia. The offerings at the shrines were carefully graded consonant with their relative importance in the eyes of the shrine-gadding world: Walsingham (half a mark or 6s 8d, 80 pence), Sudbury (half a crown or 2s 6d, 30 pence), Woolpit (20 pence), Ipswich (a quarter-mark, 3s 4d, 40 pence) and Stoke-by-Clare (20 pence). So Ipswich rated half Walsingham's offering, but outstripped the offering to the images at Sudbury, Woolpit and Stoke.[23]

At the end of the fifteenth century, only three years before the royal chaplain's visit, an Ipswich layman took a particular interest in the shrine: he was William Mynot, a clothier of St Matthew's parish, who made his will in 1499, proved the same year.[24] Mynot, who was evidently originally from Dedham in Essex, required burial before the shrine chapel door, beside another existing grave for William Saye. It is unusual to find a shrine chapel with a right of burial, but All Saints had once ranked as a parish church rather than a chapel of ease to St Matthew, and we have already seen its churchyard mentioned ninety years before Mynot made his will. Mynot also left money for images of his forbears in the east window of the chapel, and of himself and his wife in the west window (presumably as praying figures in association with devotional subjects which his executors already knew about). That might be an indication that no recent alterations had been done to the main fabric, and that the shrine chapel, despite its papal encouragement at the beginning of the cult, was a relatively modest building, still perhaps structurally mostly early Norman, and so it was now capable of being given a new appearance.

More interestingly, Mynot's bequest for new windows to commemorate his family in Gracechurch in such key positions as the east and west windows shows that in his time, the chapel was not dominated by the memorials or symbols of any other families. So it was possible for it to become visually dominated by remembrances of a man who was not of any importance in the town's hierarchy; Mynot, a newcomer to Ipswich, never held any major office in the town. That is further presumptive evidence that despite one royal visit and occasional royal interest, the Gracechurch cult had not attained more than secondary significance in Ipswich. Mynot further left a relatively modest sum to a building scheme at Gracechurch which was evidently already in train: this was for the construction of a porch 'for pour pepil to sit in', and in which his gravestone would be situated; he cited a similar existing burial site for one of his relatives in Dedham church porch. It is tempting to associate all this activity with the corporation's lease in 1497 to John Bridges, who may be identical to the chaplain of Gracechurch John Brigges who died in 1516, of a long and narrow strip of town land in the parish of St Matthew (nine feet by sixty-six feet), at 2d a year. Bridges wanted a path to his house, which was just built: perhaps a path to a new house is another indication of work being done to expand the infrastructure of Gracechurch.[25]

A new rector: Dr John Bailey

At the beginning of the sixteenth century, the pace of events at the shrine quickened and in the second decade, turned to high drama. One of the symptoms was the return to Ipswich in 1510 of a distinguished local boy who had entered the Church and made a university career. That outline profile might suggest a certain Thomas Wolsey, but Wolsey was not unique: he had an exact local contemporary in the shape of Dr John Bailey, and the two men would have known each other well. Bailey started slightly higher up the social hierarchy than Wolsey: his father Richard, of the parish of St Margaret, with substantial property also in St Clement's, had twice been bailiff of Ipswich. John Bailey's brother Robert was also a priest, and became one of the Fellows at Suffolk's important chantry college of Our Lady at Mettingham, one of whose Masters, Richard Weybread, was a close relative of the Baileys.[26] By the time Richard Bailey made his will in

1505, his son John was already 'Master' John Bailey and at some stage soon after that before his institution, he became a DD. He was born in the mid-1470s, to judge by the fact that he was elected Fellow of Pembroke Hall, Cambridge, in 1498; Wolsey was born just a few years earlier, in 1470 or 1471.[27] Bailey studied abroad for several years during his Pembroke Fellowship, and he was one of the benefactors of Gonville Hall, Cambridge, whose master William Buckenham he went on to make one of his executors. He was ordained priest in 1502, four years after Wolsey, on the title of his Fellowship of Pembroke.

Dr Bailey's father was five years dead when on 10 August 1510 King Henry VIII presented the Cambridge don to St Matthew's parish, on the death of the previous incumbent (unfortunately unnamed); he was instituted on 29 November.[28] This hardly represented a homecoming to Suffolk of a stranger after long absence: John was already much involved in the affairs of Mettingham College alongside his brother Robert.[29] Richard Braunch, Weybread's predecessor as Master of Mettingham, had made a substantial bequest in his will of 1507 to finance Dr Bailey in preaching a series of sermons in towns and villages throughout Norfolk and Suffolk.[30] Bailey was named to make his own contribution to the loan of 1522 for the French War: he was the only parish clergyman in Suffolk with the misfortune to have sufficient independent means to be included in this list.[31]

All this gives us the picture of a cleric who possessed wealth, cosmopolitan experience, charisma and widely-based local influence. Despite Bailey's eminence in Cambridge University and his continuing association with Pembroke and Gonville Hall, he proved himself deeply committed to his parish after 1510; not all Cambridge dons were so assiduous in their benefices at the time. His will shows that he was resident in the parish, that he had made St Matthew his 'avower' or patron saint, and that he insisted on burial in the most prominent place in St Matthew's church before the high altar; the indent of his monumental brass, with effigy, inscription, chalice and four corner symbols, was still visible there in the nineteenth century.[32] It is interesting that when Bailey named his chief executor as Dr William Buckenham, he described his fellow-Cambridge don in reference to Buckenham's benefice of St Michael Coslany in Norwich, rather than giving him his title of Master of Gonville Hall, Cambridge: perhaps their parishes mattered more to both of them than Cambridge, but certainly St Matthew's mattered more to Dr Bailey.

Why should such a man come to St Matthew's? Certainly the wealth of the benefice was appropriate for a high-flyer in the Church, but that was also its problem: St Matthew's was precisely the sort of parish which was scooped up by pluralist clergy who would rarely take an interest in it and put in curates to do the actual work. Two examples stand out among Bailey's fifteenth-century predecessors: first and most spectacularly, Robert Booth or Bothe, Rector of St Matthew's from 1473 to 1476 – his first living (of many) after being priested. Booth was well-connected: the illegitimate son of a knight as well as being nephew to Archbishop Booth of York. In 1479, slightly belatedly, he regularised his various extensive ecclesiastical offices including his former possession of St Matthew's, two years after rather predictably becoming Dean of York Minster, while making sure through two successive papal dispensations that he could continue to hold up to two parish benefices if he wanted to.[33]

Booth's successor Edward or Edmund Assheton, who was maybe Bailey's immediate predecessor as rector, was a canon lawyer like Booth, and when admitted in 1476, he only held 'the first tonsure'; in other words, he was not yet a priest.[34] Also like Booth, in 1494 Assheton sought and obtained a dispensation from Rome to receive and retain for life two extra benefices in addition to the benefice of St Matthew's, or without it, three. He was from a prominent knightly family of Middleton (Lancs), and became incumbent there two years after his papal dispensation for pluralism, and that was presumably the main aim of obtaining the dispensation.[35] Clearly it was that rich family benefice in Lancashire which chiefly interested Assheton, and that was where eventually he became a resident parish priest; he frequently presided in person over the Court Baron of Middleton, and was buried in Middleton Church with a fine monumental brass in 1522.[36]

Bailey, by contrast to these aristocratic high-flying careerists, became (as we have seen) an enthusiastically resident rector at St Matthew's, and he does not seem to have sought any other cure of souls; moreover, he was a theologian by university training, unlike the canon lawyers Bothe and Assheton, whose training would naturally pull them towards senior church administration rather than to pastoral ministry in a parish. The continuing residence of this distinguished cleric in the parish would represent something new in its parochial life, let alone the town as a whole, which was not to boast any resident clergyman of equivalent stature till the Protestant establishment of a borough lecturership in the reign of Elizabeth I. St Matthew's was not the parish where Bailey had grown up, and it did not feature in his father's will. It may be significant that his return to

Ipswich occurred at much the same time as the spectacular benefaction instituted in the parish of St Matthew by one of Ipswich's wealthiest men, Edmund Daundy. This was the foundation of Daundy's set of fifteen almshouses, which were sited in Lady Lane, seven one side, eight the other, abutting on to the site of the shrine itself.

Daundy had already founded these some time before his death in 1515, and as the reader will by now appreciate, they were actually a refoundation, for the western block occupied the same site which was previously occupied by St John's Hospital or almshouse, with its modest endowment of a field to its south. Their rebuilding on the site to the south of Gracechurch represented a major upgrade of the cluster of sacred buildings at the West Gate of the town, for any almshouse was a factory of prayers sent up to Heaven by its putatively grateful inhabitants. The number fifteen might indeed have been a reminiscence of the 'Fifteen Oes of St Bridget', a distinctively English devotion, which Eamon Duffy has called 'probably the most popular of all prayers in late medieval England', and which was intimately associated with the cult of Purgatory.[37]

While leaving nothing at all to St Matthew's Church in his will (which was made in 1515 and proved the following year), Edmund Daundy clearly conceived his almshouses as an integral part of the shrine complex of Gracechurch.[38] In fact in his will, he said so, calling them his almshouses 'besides Our Lady of Grace', when he left provision for firewood for the inhabitants. The will shows him otherwise to be a generous benefactor of his own town-centre parish church of St Lawrence, the saint whom he chose as his 'avower', and he made provision for splendid tombs for himself and his first wife in the chancel there. By contrast, the almshouses played no apparent part in the foundation of Daundy's elaborate new chantry foundation of St Thomas Becket in St Lawrence's Church, and they were not mentioned at all in the royal mortmain licence for the chantry which was granted on 29 December 1509. This was just as well, since amid the great dissolutions of the Reformation, somehow the borough was able to get away with pretending that the almshouses had never had a superstitious purpose. In Daundy's will, they were discussed separately from his provision for the chantry. That suggests a separate motive for this foundation at Gracechurch. In any case, it represented a promotion for the shrine, and that might require a clergyman of much greater status than previous incumbents of St Matthew's to give general oversight to the growing complex. Who might fit all these pieces together?

We should note that Edmund Daundy was uncle to Thomas Wolsey – his sister Joan was Wolsey's mother. Wolsey, the former Oxford don, was now outstripping his Cambridge contemporary Dr Bailey in his rise in the Church. From November 1509 he was almoner to King Henry VIII; Bailey's acquisition of the royal parish of St Matthew though came ten months later, in August 1510, and was surely the result of Wolsey's patronage. We might see his appointment as the first visible sign of Wolsey's interest in Gracechurch, which might also have inspired Daundy to found his almshouses there. Altogether, there was a new bustle and prominence for the shrine, which was now to have a dramatic and unexpected consequence: exactly the sort of wondrous event which over the last millennium, had come to characterise Marian shrines right across Europe. In its spectacular character, it was the equal of the less well-documented miracles at the time of the cult's inauguration in the 1320s. Repeatedly, such occurrences involve people without the normal resources of worldly power, either children or women. In this case, it was a girl, though unusually, not a girl of humble circumstances, but the daughter of a prominent Essex knight.

Above: Curson Lodge on the corner of Silent Street and St Nicholas Street, its extent defined by the mullioned windows and exposed timber-framing. The corner post has a most interesting Merchant's Mark which has so far defied interpretation. This 15th century building will have been convenient lodging for Curson's retainers when he was entertaining first the queen in 1517 and then the king three years later. Their large retinues will have displaced Curson's, indeed the lesser royal servants may also have overflowed to stay in the lodge. The Wentworths may have stayed with the Cursons or in the Lodge; the account of the miracles makes it clear that the Maid could summon Lord and Lady Curson immediately and at any hour, implying that she was no further away from the Curson mansion than the lodge. On the left of the photograph, just out of shot, stands Cardinal House, the modern premises of Ensors. This was built on the site of Robert Wolsey's tavern and butchery and there Thomas Wolsey lived from the age of two or three when the family migrated here from the Elms parish until he went up to Oxford.

Opposite: Sir Robert, Lord Curson's late 15th century mansion is here reconstructed from a Tudor plan by Bill Haward (BL Cotton Augustus MS I, vol 2, No 48). The very detailed plan was almost certainly commissioned for Wolsey when he was planning to retire there. The two-storey porch was tall enough to admit a horse and rider and stood where Wolsey's statue sits today. The first court had a great parlour to the north and a smaller one to the south. The buttery was on the corner of Rose Lane, and the chapel to the east had a raised family pew on the south cloister side. There was a dove house in the courtyard beyond the chapel. Most of the service rooms ran north from the gatehouse tower along Silent Street, over which lay the Lodge (above) where the Maid probably had her lodgings during the events of 1516.

Wonders and miracles: the Maid of Ipswich

There is a wealth of information to triangulate the story of what happened, but the central source is quite out of the ordinary: an eye-witness account by a man at the centre of events.[39] Moreover it was personally addressed apparently to King Henry VIII himself, but possibly alternatively to either Cardinal Wolsey or the Dukes of Suffolk or Norfolk, in the form of a briefing paper or memorandum.[40] The author was no less a person than an Imperial count, Sir Robert (styled Lord) Curson, who at the time was Ipswich's most socially-elevated resident, living in semi-retirement in the town's grandest house after a somewhat murky military and political career. Curson, for all the hard-nosed politics on which his eminence was based (or perhaps precisely because of that) was sucked in to the drama until he became one of its leading actors, maybe initially simply because his house was both the most appropriately impressive near to the shrine. For whatever reason, he became impresario and chronicler of the proceedings, alongside Dr John Bailey of St Matthew's church. It all began in November 1515 in north Essex near Thaxted, as the twelve-year old daughter of Sir Roger Wentworth of Gosfield (twice MP for Ipswich in the 1480s) started suffering violent fits. These went on tormenting her till the following Lady Day (25 March 1516), when a persistent vision of the Virgin 'in the picture and stature of our Lady of Grace in Eppeswyche' for the time being put an end to her trouble.

The girl nevertheless insisted on being taken to Ipswich, rejecting all suggestions of other possible Our Ladies, and three weeks later, on Sunday 13 April 1516 (the MS mistakenly makes this 14 April), she was ceremoniously escorted to the chapel, and after many fits, regained 'here ryght schape and was a fayre cretoure'. Over the next days, as news travelled fast along Suffolk's main roads leading away from the gates of Ipswich, more than a thousand people came to witness her anarchically pious activities, which culminated in the girl summoning Curson and the town bailiffs to pray for her, saying 'it was our ladys wylle'. On that Tuesday, the county's most powerful cleric, Abbot John Reve *alias* Melford, arrived from his Abbey of St Edmund, having travelled the thirty miles from Bury on foot 'of pylgremage'; the crowds in the chapel were so great that Curson could hardly push a way through for the Abbot to say mass. Reve, fortified by a good dinner at the Curson mansion, then pressed on to visit the Good Rood of Dovercourt in north-east Essex, vowing to repeat his Ipswich pilgrimage yearly if Our Lady would effect a cure for the girl. Cured she duly was, and she led the crowd in prayer, promising to return to Ipswich in eleven days.

Alas, the girl's parents decided to delay this return till Whitsun (11 May 1516), ostensibly to provide time to gather 'the most worschipfull of the contrey', but perhaps feeling that she had had enough excitement for the time being – one of the many indications that at this stage, the Wentworth family found the whole business deeply embarrassing, and were not as convinced as those who did not know the girl so well, of the genuinely spiritual quality of her performances. The result was a set of renewed tantrums and fits which forced her parents into agreeing to her return to Ipswich a week before Whitsun; the chosen day was now Thursday 1 May 1516, with appropriate symbolism, since it was both Ascension Day and the beginning of Mary's month of May. That ensured an even greater crowd to receive her at Gracechurch: the turnout was estimated by Curson to be four thousand, and included the leading knights and clergy of the shire.

The girl did her devotions at the shrine and admonished the crowd to be 'more stedfast in the fayth' before retiring for the night, but at midnight she suddenly summoned the bailiffs of Ipswich, county JPs, Dr Bailey and other worthies to her lodgings. She then launched on a two-hour sermon, showing scant respect for the clergy's conventional and adult learning, and gave a sharp response to her mother's admonition 'A [Ah] dowther ye must take hede to the grette clerkes and of ther sayyng'; she emphasised her retort by falling into another fit. Curson successfully brought that to an end by thrusting his cross decorated with a Pièta into her hands, but an hour later, she began taking her revenge on previously sceptical siblings: her sisters and a cousin burst from their beds in a demented state. Cured in their turn by her ministrations, they gave place to her brother John, whom she cured of two raving and blasphemous fits, the second before the image of Our Lady in the shrine itself. After this night of excitement, Dr Bailey brought the proceedings to a decorous end on the following Sunday afternoon (4 May 1516) with an edifying sermon, obviously delighted that his own shrine had witnessed such an event that 'syth that England was crystened were never schewed suche meracles.'

The dramatic saga would have figured very neatly as an addition to the catalogue of miracles in Wynkyn de Worde's compilation at substantial length, *The myracles of our lady*, which was popular enough to go through three surviving editions in 1496, 1514 and 1530, possibly with others which have not survived. De Worde did not in fact draw on it to expand his later editions, but his best-seller had helped to create the climate of devotion in which the events of 1516 made perfect sense to the crowds which experienced

them, let alone to the teenager who was the principal performer. The Maid would have been well-primed if her family had a well-thumbed copy of de Worde's publication, or indeed, if they had just acquired the latest edition on the eve of her troubles in 1516. She may well have read with fascination (or more likely, heard read to her), such stories as de Worde's 'How this holy name Maria put the devyl a waye', a stirring little tale in which certain Spanish monks found that the name of Mary drove the devil from their window when the names of the Trinity, the Passion narrative, the seven penitential psalms and holy water had all failed to do so.[41]

Woodcut from Wynkyn de Worde's *The myracles of our lady* of which there were three editions between 1496 and 1530. The Wentworth girl may been familiar with this strong image. At the foot of the composition, Jesse lies asleep, and from his side springs a sturdy wooden stem branching to support some of his descendants. King David plays his harp on the right and higher up there are several kings holding sceptres. Mary and the Child spring from the root of Jesse as predicted in Isaiah Chapter 11. On the left level with the Virgin's halo kneels St James the Great wearing his large-brimmed hat and a quatrefoil intended for his traditional scallop shell.

It was very soon after these events that Lord Curson sat down to capture it all, writing away, he says, until he had used up all his available parchment. The account which we have is not Curson's original but a contemporary manuscript copy tipped into the back of a much earlier book from Reading Abbey which is a collection of ecclesiastical histories and historical lists, now in the British Library. The Reading text is in a small neat secretary hand, yet it is manifestly secondary because of its omissions, mis-readings and insertions of words, and it was probably copied from a printed version of Curson's account, since in 1520, the Oxford bookseller John Dorne was offering for sale a pamphlet entitled 'The miracke of oure lady Ipsiiwise'. That is surely identifiable with this text; its price of twopence sounds right for the length.[42] So a monk of Reading is likely to have been excited by the story after he had borrowed the pamphlet from a friend and written it out for his own edification.[43]

The immediate sensation of the events was perhaps all too much for two pious elderly inhabitants of St Matthew's parish, hastening their departure to a more face-to-face meeting with Our Lady. One of them was John Smith, a pewterer, whose will, made only two days before his death on 18 May 1516 (only a fortnight after Dr Bailey's sermon), reveals that he lived very close to the shrine, in a house 'without the Bargate'. We know when he died because it was formerly recorded on the back of a choir-stall in St Matthew's, alas now destroyed; it is not especially common for a date of death to be recorded in this manner.[44] The priest John Brigges made his will four days after Smith's death, on 22 May 1516, with bequests to John Master, Bailey's veteran curate at St Matthew's; these suggest that Brigges was the chaplain of Gracechurch. He demanded burial within the shrine chapel, and he soon got his wish, to judge by the will's probate date of 3 July 1516.[45] Nor was the miracle of 1516 a mere nine-days' wonder. In 1529 Sir Thomas More used Curson's account, no doubt simply by reading its printed pamphlet version, which would have provided all but one of the details in the substantial description of events which he gave in his *Dialogue concerning Heresies*. More was defending the Gracechurch miracle against sneers which his evangelical opponent William Tyndale had previously made in the course of Tyndale's *Obedience of a Christian Man*, published in 1527. Far from giving any ground to Tyndale's scepticism, More cited the activities of little Mistress Wentworth as the best modern example of a miracle in England.[46]

The clash between Tyndale and More in 1529 was addressed to a reading public which would still be very familiar with the events of thirteen years before, not merely because of the presence of thousands at the original events, but also thanks to the further publicity afforded by visits to Gracechurch from the greatest in the kingdom. First, in 1517 came Queen Katherine of Aragon and Cardinal Wolsey, and later, in 1522, the King himself. The reasonably detailed account of the Queen's visit we possess, in a stray from the borough archives in the British Library, makes it very clear how much her time in the town was focussed on the shrine and on Lord Curson, the nobleman who had described the miracle for the King.

The Queen arrived on Thursday 2 April 1517 and was escorted by the Bailiffs and Portmen from 'Brookishallefeld'. Brokes Hall was the Ipswich mansion of the prominent courtier, Sir Anthony Wingfield of Letheringham, Curson's only possible rival as a local resident with the status of a courtier; it stood just north of what is now a double roundabout on the junction of the Norwich/Yarmouth Road and Valley Road, in other words, three-quarters of a mile north-west of Gracechurch. The Queen's procession took her straight along to the shrine and then to Lord Curson's house, where she was to stay, no doubt eagerly hearing his own account of the wonders: maybe it was at her prompting that Curson wrote his narrative. She was back at Gracechurch on Friday for a series of masses before a procession as far as Cornhill, and then without further ado, the royal exit took place over Bourn Bridge, south through Essex to London.[47]

Wolsey left his visit to Ipswich till September that year. As he announced to the King in a letter at the beginning of the month, this journey to Norfolk and Suffolk was both intended to remedy his ill-health, and to fulfill a vow he had made.[48] This was the Cardinal's first major return to his birthplace during the years of his greatness, and it was sourly remembered by his enemies a decade later as one of the leading occasions on which he had publicly 'triumphed'.[49] Certainly it constituted a major progress right across East Anglia, befitting a papal legate rather than a Lord Chancellor. It began as far away from Ipswich as the other Marian shrine at Walsingham, which was conveniently at the other outer edge of the East Anglian region from Ipswich, enabling Wolsey to take in as much of his native country as possible (one notes that just as in the mind of Hugh Latimer and Elizabeth of York's accountants, Our Lady of Walsingham took precedence in the Cardinal's plans over Our Lady of Ipswich). Wolsey's route took in Abbot Reve's monastery at Bury St Edmunds, where he brusquely sided with that co-star of the Gracechurch miracle against local opponents of the Abbot's jurisdiction.[50]

Finally, on 8 October 1522, Henry VIII arrived in the town and stayed overnight with Curson at his mansion. Almost as soon as he had risen, he paid a visit to the shrine and made his offering there. Reversing the itinerary followed by Wolsey, he then headed north into Norfolk to Walsingham, before returning to his Essex palace of New Hall at Boreham.[51] The future looked bright for Our Lady of Ipswich. It is difficult not to think that the events aided the grant of a new royal charter to the borough in 1519, confirming rights granted by an unfortunately mislaid charter from Edward IV.[52] Sir Roger Wentworth, now resigned to his daughter's celebrity, was still maintaining two priests to serve the chapel when it was dissolved in 1538, a year before his own death; it would have been a considerable compensation for the Maid's highhanded treatment of her parents that her brother John entered Cardinal Wolsey's service at some point after the Gracechurch miracle.[53] Nor can Sir Robert Curson have felt dissatisfied with the consequences of the Maid's wonders: he became host successively to the Queen and the King, confirming his already senior status in the county and his place in national life. In the 1530s, he was among those who not only gave but received New Year's gifts from the King.[54]

Woodcut of about 1490 showing pilgrims of the ordinary sort. They are warmly clad and stoutly shod, and carry something with which to defend themselves if necessary. Their broad-brimmed hats are decorated with souvenirs of the shrines they have been to, but none with any certain connection with the Ipswich shrine have been identified. Badges were cast in lead or pewter in shallow moulds at most shrines and it would be surprising if none were offered for sale here in Ipswich. Lead ampullae made to hold oil or holy water are known with a crowned Lombardic letter I, but that is more likely to mean Jesus (ihesus) than Ipswich. Pilgrims often wore their badges until they next crossed or arrived at the bank of a river, when by casting them into the water the benefit of their visit to the shrine was thought to be enhanced. The banks of the Thames have yielded quantities of pilgrim badges to metal detectorists.

In these boom years for the shrine, at least four hostelries made a direct pitch for the less spiritual needs of the pilgrims who came to Gracechurch, theming themselves as places of entertainment and hospitality in such circumstances. At the east of the town at the far end of Carr Street (Caristrete) there was, and is, the Salutation. The name is a clear association with Gabriel's greeting to Mary at the Annunciation, and one might also read the

Annunciation into the name of another inn, the Angel, on the corner of Great Bolton (or St George's) Street and Clay Lane, which retained its name until 1610. Abutting the Westgate on its north side in St Matthew's Street, diagonally opposite from the shrine itself, was the Three Kings, and in the eighteenth century, its sign board (like that of the Three Feathers opposite, on the south side of St Matthew's Street) hung out across the way from Norwich and Bury St Edmunds into the main street of the town. Anyone walking from the Salutation to the Three Kings had travelled the Nativity story from beginning to end: a fine festive pilgrimage across the borough. The Assumption Inn was early and important, probably not far along Gaolgate Lane from the gate. In 1528 its proprietor was prepared to pay sixpence a year to be allowed to hoist his sign on a pole set in Corporation ground, in order that it would be seen at a greater distance. That was the year that Cardinal College seal was designed showing the same event in the life of the Virgin, but like the College, the inn was destined to disappear or change its name after the 1530s, becoming the Chequers. That there were three or four hostelries named in honour of the Blessed Virgin Mary and ready to greet pilgrims to the shrine is surely an indication that many people came from a distance while the shrine operated.[55]

Protestants themselves obliquely recognised the power of the Gracechurch events in the abuse which they heaped on them, extending over half-century from William Tyndale's first literary polemic in 1527. They seized repeatedly on the demonic character of the girl's fits which was already avowedly a theme in Robert Curson's narrative, and they frequently and understandably linked this 'Maid of Ipswich' with Elizabeth Barton the 'Maid of Kent'. Barton's trances and inspired traditionalist prophecies began a decade later than Mistress Wentworth's, and may well have been inspired by her knowledge of the Ipswich events; like Wentworth's demonstrations, they were publicized in a printed pamphlet which (also like Curson's) does not now exist in its original form, and they attracted an equally significant audience among both ordinary people and the great and the good. Because Barton had the misfortune to come to national attention amid the full flood of the early English Reformation, she assumed huge political significance during the King's break with Rome, and was executed for treason in 1534.[56]

Scornful Protestant descriptions of the Maid of Ipswich provide us with further independent if not always reliable details about the events of 1516. First, the historian and evangelical polemicist John Bale, in a characteristically bilious work published in 1545, made a further bitter but very significant passing remark about Gracechurch, which throws the spotlight back on to Dr John Bailey: 'Doctor Baylye in Sothfolke wroughte great myracles by syr Roger Wenforthes dowter to auaunce the great ladye of Ippeswyche.'[57] Bailey's alleged deception formed the first in Bale's formidable list of deceitful clerics promoting traditional religion over the following quarter century. Bale was a Suffolk man by birth; he spent some time in Ipswich in the early 1530s while still a Carmelite friar, before his conversion to the evangelical cause, and later that decade, he was back in the county as a curate and protégé of Sir Roger's Wentworth's evangelical cousin Thomas Lord Wentworth. So Bale remained close to events in Ipswich, and this remark in 1545 was not his first reference to the shrine, as we will see (below, p. 56). He was evidently drawing on local knowledge in this perception that the Gracechurch miracle was a vital stage in the promotion of the shrine. Bailey cannot have organised a manipulative teenager into having pubertal hysterics, but he can probably be given the credit for raising the profile of his shrine to the extent that it caught the imagination of an Essex girl, and certainly he took charge in a way that would make the most dramatic sense out of the potentially chaotic events.

The Maid's first name: Jane or Anne?

Protestant polemics may also shed light on the question of the Maid's Christian name. It was odd that Curson and therefore More had not given their readers this, perhaps because the Maid had insisted on going into anonymity in a nunnery. That was the one extra fact which More did add to Curson's account – indeed it was the only detail which he could not have derived from the eye-witness account in Curson's pamphlet. More said that the Maid had joined the 'mynoresse', which has always been taken to refer to the London house of Franciscan nuns or Poor Clares, the Minories, a house which More had long known well – but Richard Rex was the first to point out that it might equally apply to a Suffolk house of Poor Clares, the Minoresses of Bruisyard. At its dissolution, Bruisyard had a nun called Dame Jane Wentworth, who made her will as late as 1565 (it was proved in 1572).[58]

There are nevertheless problems with this very beguiling identification. Margery Calthorpe, penultimate Abbess of Bruisyard, did indeed have close Wentworth kin, but they were from the senior line at Nettlestead near Ipswich rather than their Gosfield Wentworth cousins, who had moved to Essex in the mid-fifteenth century, and a Nettlestead connection could account for a Jane Wentworth among Margery

Calthorpe's nuns.[59] There was indeed a Jane Wentworth in the Nettlestead family who was alive and unmarried in 1501, and who could therefore have survived until 1572.[60] When Jane Wentworth made her will in 1565, she made the main beneficiary and executor Sir Robert Wingfield, one of the most active in the forward Protestant party among the Suffolk magistracy, who was closely allied by his marriage into the Nettlestead Wentworths and shared their pronounced and precocious Protestantism, while he was not related to their Gosfield cousins. Jane made a point of asking for burial in Framlingham parish church, beside the 'stool' where she had been accustomed to sit. This ex-nun does not sound like an out-and-out recusant, and seems to have travelled far from the extrovert Marian devotion which had characterised the events of 1516. Sir Robert Wingfield would have been Jane's great-nephew via his wife Dame Cecily Wentworth from the Nettlestead family, to whom Jane left a prettily-decorated counterpane – that is, if this Jane is to be identified with Jane Wentworth of Nettlestead, rather than one of the Wentworths of Gosfield.[61]

Sir Roger Wentworth of Gosfield is not recorded as having a daughter called Jane – but neither does he appear in the family pedigree with a daughter called Anne, which is the only near-contemporary attribution of a Christian name to the Maid of Ipswich.[62] That occurs in the theological notebooks of Archbishop Thomas Cranmer from the late 1530s, in a context whose reliability is rather undermined by its previous missnaming of the Maid of Kent as Agnes rather than Elizabeth. The name Anne is repeated in a printed work derived from Cranmer's same notebooks and published by Marian Protestant exiles in Wesel in 1556. This adds the intriguing details, which convincingly overlap with Curson's account, that the Maid 'tolde many men the secretes of their hertes / which they thoughte no man could haue tolde but god only: she cut stomagers [stomachers] in peces & made them whole againe / & caused diuerse men / that spake agaynst her delusions / to goe starke mad.'[63] It is also clear that John Bale, the Suffolk Protestant who might have been more likely than Cranmer's circle to know the Christian name of the Maid of Ipswich, did not, for as we have seen, in 1545 he simply referred to her as 'syr Roger Wenforthes dowter'.

Alas, therefore, the identity of the Wentworth Maid of Ipswich must remain open between a Jane and an Anne. Yet another daughter of Sir Roger Wentworth, Ursula, became a nun, in her case at Essex's ancient Benedictine abbey at Barking. Her choice of convent rules her out as a candidate for the Maid of Ipswich, since More, writing in 1529, would not have mistaken that great monastic house for one of the Minoress convents, but we can hazard that it was the events of 1516 starring the Maid that had inspired Ursula to take the veil. She was one of those sisters who despite their initial scepticism, had been drawn into the Maid's powerful performance, and clearly the effect had been lasting, although one notes that she did not choose to join her sister at a Minoress House. Ursula was at Barking at least by 1527, eleven years after her part in the events at Gracechurch, for in that year she took part in the election of the next Abbess, her cousin Dorothy Barley (the Barking nuns included a strong element of closely-related East Anglian gentlewomen; via her mother Anne Tyrrell, Ursula Wentworth was also a relative of the Prioress, Mary Tyrell).

Making her will at the end of Queen Mary I's reign at Shellow Bowels in Essex, Ursula Wentworth showed more overt traditional piety than Jane Wentworth of Framlingham was to do. She left money for masses, months-minds and obits, and she had kept close after the dissolution to one of the other former nuns of Barking, Margery Ballard, to whom she bequeathed clothing, a valuable parsonage lease and (interestingly) her 'Latin books'.[64] Ex-Abbess Barley of Barking, whose will was proved in 1559, the same year as Ursula's, bequeathed Wentworth 'a tablet of mother of Pearle enclosing ii Images of sylver and gylt': just the sort of object which Lord Curson had used to cure the Maid of Ipswich's fit back in 1516.[65] This continuing circle of devout and well-educated ladies with their multiple family connections was thus still in touch with the lush Catholic piety which had nurtured the Gracechurch miracles.

Eight years after Ursula's will, with the new Protestant dispensation of Queen Elizabeth increasingly securely in place, Sir John Wentworth, son of Sir Roger and brother to both Ursula and the Maid, made his will, on 8 October 1566. He was much more tight-lipped about religion, even though long before, he had been a servant of Cardinal Wolsey (so, of course, had been the shrine's nemesis, Thomas Cromwell). Yet in 1564 Sir John Wentworth had been described as a 'hinderer' of religion in Essex by Edmund Grindal, Bishop of London, when the Bishop sent in his county return for a nationwide survey of religious opinion among Justices of the Peace commissioned by the Privy Council.[66] Although Wentworth's will reveals nothing overt to mark him out as the sympathizer with Catholicism whom Grindal had described, it describes financial and property dealings with East Anglian magnate relatives who were likewise outwardly conforming to the Elizabethan Settlement, while being in reality less than positively enthusiastic for Protestantism: principally William Waldegrave of Bures and Sir William Cordell of Long Melford. Very significant also was Wentworth's choice of executor alongside his wife: his cousin Rooke Green of Little Sampford, also in Essex, and not far from Gosfield. Green was soon to emerge in mid-Elizabethan Essex as a firm Catholic recusant.[67] A more startling fact about Mr Green brings us full circle to the Maid and the events of 1516: his step-mother Margaret was actually the widow of Sir Robert Curson, Curson's much younger second wife, who had remarried Rooke Green's father Sir Edward Green, and we will return to a consequence of that connection below.[68]

Yet another daughter of Sir Roger Wentworth can probably (fortunately) be ruled out as a candidate for the Maid: Laura, who married the Essex gentleman Edmund Shaa of Horndon-on-the Hill. An alarming and alas undated document among Cardinal Wolsey's papers, probably from the 1520s, details her escapades with Edward Bugges, steward to her husband: 'all the cunntry spekith shame of them boothe', it records. This was the household from Hell, revolving round what sounds like Shaa's mental or physical incapacity, since Laura and Bugges frequently locked him in one of the rooms of the house and returned spirited insults to Laura's father Sir Roger Wentworth when he ordered Bugges to leave his daughter's company. Laura would bully Shaa into signing legal documents and when she was too 'oversen with drynke that she can neyther goo nor stond', Bugges would carry her to bed. Only his twelve-year-old daughter was available to attend her, after another of her attendants had effectively accused the unruly couple of adultery. It sounds as if the family tensions evident in the Maid's fits and exhibitions had affected this particular sister in a very different manner.[69]

A witness to the wonders: St Matthew's font

It is the visits to Ipswich of the King, Queen and Papal Legate in the decade after the Maid's demonstrations that have prompted the present authors to look afresh at the magnificent font in Dr Bailey's parish church of St Matthew, now standing in the north aisle after more than one move in its history. In basic form, it is the usual octagonal bowl on octagonal stem which one expects from the Perpendicular period, but the stem is ingeniously caused by the eight figures surrounding it to sit on a square base, with the eight figures standing on square blocks like crenellations, so that the whole composition of the font appears to be based on the top of a parapetted tower, or even the aftercastle of a ship (which would suggest an allusion to the borough arms of Ipswich).

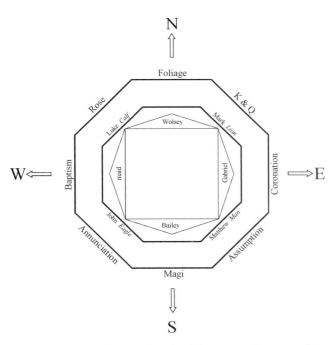

N

Foliage

Rose

K & Q

Luke *Calf*

Wolsey

Mark *Lion*

maid

Gabriel

Baptism

W

Coronation

E

John *Eagle*

Bailey

Matthew *Man*

Annunciation

Assumption

Magi

S

E

Above that very individual feature, the rest of the detail makes the font one of the most unusual in East Anglia. It resembles in form and the richness of the figures in its panels the seven sacrament fonts of which there are twenty-two in Norfolk and fourteen in Suffolk, and it may be from the same workshop as some of them, but the iconography of the composition is completely different and without exact parallel. One of the most remarkable things about it is that it is in perfect order, free from damage and with minimal Victorian restoration. Its exuberant devotional imagery would surely have been a prime target for iconoclasts such as William Dowsing on his visit on 29 January 1644 during his extended East Anglian campaigns of destruction.[70] The font is a very bulky object to have been stowed out of sight at any period, and the only credible explanation of its present condition is that early in the Reformation, its panels were filled with plaster, as is known to have been the case for other Suffolk fonts. The uncovering would have been done before 1824, when D.E. Davy provided a succinct description of what can be seen today, but it was remembered by Wodderspoon, who said in 1850 that 'This font occupied for many years an almost hidden position, and the designs were blocked up by mortar and masonry.' He also added that '[t]he carving has been cleaned and the figures retouched by chisel', but that does not suggest extensive damage needing repair.[71]

Around the stem are the symbolic winged figures of the four evangelists, the man of St Matthew to the south east, then, anticlockwise, the lion of St Mark, these two with scrolls, the calf of St Luke and the eagle of St John, neither having scrolls. These alternate with

four individually-characterised figures. To the east there is an angel; his hands are broken off, but perhaps originally he held a scroll with the message of the Annunciation ('Hail Mary, full of grace'). Then, anticlockwise, there is a priest wearing a cap with tassels hanging behind his shoulders, holding two objects, the right-hand of which seems rectilinear or box-like in shape. Then follows a female in civilian clothes, bareheaded, with her hair falling loose (hence a young unmarried woman), her right hand raised to bless, and fourthly, there is a priest without tonsure holding two objects, both roughly spherical, but one elongated in the vertical axis. Once more, as in the case of the other priest, neither of these objects resembles a chalice or paten. Both priests wear alb and chasuble.

Above the stem, the octagonal bowl is supported by busts of eight angels, their wings overlapping. Of the main panels, two are filled with plant designs, but the other six consist of scenes under double canopies. The designs from the north, anti-clockwise, are:

1. A quadripartite foliage design springing from a central spiral

2. A rose of five petals, with four outer petals and two small extra petals at the foot, making six petals on the outer flower

3. The Baptism of Christ, with John the Baptist at left in a long robe, Christ at the right in the water, the Baptist holding an object intended to hold water, perhaps a large shell, centrally above them both

4. The Annunciation, with a pot of lilies between the angel Gabriel and the Virgin. Given that she is depicted prior to the birth of Christ, she is not crowned, but the dove of the spirit, flying from the end of a scroll held by Gabriel, is whispering his message in her right ear (the common medieval belief was that the conception of Jesus occurred through Mary's ear, since this was how she had heard the news, the idea conveniently pre-empting any less decorous thoughts on the part of the faithful). On her left, intruding into the pedestal of the subsidiary figure (iv below) beside her, is what may be a prayer-desk topped by a cushion: a common accompaniment in contemporary images of the Annunciation.

5. The Adoration of the Magi, two standing, one kneeling with a gift, the figures of the trio at the left separated from the Virgin and Child by a curiously large central expanse of drapery, perhaps symbolising the unveiling of Christ at the Epiphany; at top right, the heads of an ox and an ass. The Virgin is crowned.

6. The Assumption of the Virgin: the Virgin, crowned, on a radiate background within a mandorla flanked by four angels supporting the mandorla, the lower two demi-figures but of the same scale as the upper.

7. The Virgin crowned in Heaven by the Trinity, the Son (crowned and beardless) to the left, the Father (crowned and bearded) to the right, with the dove of the Holy Trinity descending on her, attached to the central crocket of the double canopy.

8. A queen (left) and king (right), both seated, with radiate glories behind either of them, and a prayer desk at the right side of each of them. Their arms and hands are in front of them, damaged and largely broken off, but neither praying nor blessing.

In a most unusual enrichment, between the eight main panels of the bowl there are tiny figures of people, male and female and mostly lay, each on a pedestal and under a crocketted canopy. In sequence anti-clockwise from the angle of the bowl between the two floriate panels, they are (i) bare-headed bearded male figure in gown gathered in folds (ii) female figure with veil headdress and gown over underskirt (iii) bearded male figure wearing a brimmed hat (iv) male figure in gown and unbrimmed hat, gown to feet in irregular swirling folds (v) bare-headed clean-shaven male figure apparently wearing a chasuble over an alb (vi) female figure with tall head-dress, in gown over under-skirt (vii) bare-headed bearded male figure in gown holding an object, perhaps a baby (viii) bare-headed clean-shaven male figure.

Five of the eight main panels are subjects taken from the 'joys of Mary', the details no doubt copied from some contemporary woodcut sequence: the Annunciation, the Nativity, the Adoration of the Magi, the Assumption and the Virgin's Coronation appear here out of a permutation of 'joys' which are commonly grouped as five, seven or occasionally fifteen. It will be noted that three of these joys, the Annunciation or Salutation, the Adoration of the Magi and the Assumption, were commemorated in the names of Ipswich taverns in the early sixteenth century. The Baptism of Christ, not normally numbered among the joys of Mary, is nevertheless appropriate to a font. The rose panel could be taken as for Mary, but in heraldry it could also serve as an introduction to the double rose of the Tudors, who are surely the subject of the sixth figural panel.

The presence of what appears to be a prayer desk beside the King in the sixth panel (though it is just possible that it is the bench on which he sits) is a good indication that this is not God the Father, who hardly needs such an accoutrement to pray to himself: the King is therefore an earthly monarch. He wears a short tunic over a long garment, and is broad-faced and bearded; we could be looking for a rough sketch of the famous Holbein portrait of Henry VIII. Beside him, unmistakeably at her prayer-desk, is his queen: Catherine of Aragon. They are not using their prayer desks, but sitting looking out at the viewer. It is perhaps unexpected that both of them are surrounded by radiate glories, which in Seven Sacrament fonts at Denston, Woodbridge and Great Glemham are the background to the sacrament panels, but what is also significant here is that in the other panels of the font, no other figure apart from the Virgin in her Assumption is thus treated: so it is the Virgin's effulgence which surrounds the King and his consort, just as it could be presumed to have done on their respective visits to Ipswich.

The lesser figures interspersing the main panels on this reading may be taken as pilgrims; one (iii) is after all wearing the brimmed hat which is so commonly the attribute of a pilgrim. It is improbable that we can do any better than that in identifying the individuals concerned, but it is not unlikely that they would have been understood as particular individuals prominent in the events around the Maid's visions; perhaps we might see the town's two annual bailiffs among them. The four figures on the stem between the four evangelistic symbols represent puzzles which offer greater possibilities of resolution. One of the two clergy is a secular priest who might well be Dr Bailey, and the other priest has headgear which with its tassels cannot be other than a rather bulky version of a cardinal's hat. The clergy do not appear to be holding chalice and paten as one would expect, but offerings. The presence of an angel paired with an unmarried young woman might suggest a second Annunciation scene, but Mary is never shown as blessing in the iconography of Annunciation groups. The risky thought occurs that the bare-headed and long-haired young woman giving a blessing, wearing the plainest of robes and no crown, is actually the Maid of Ipswich, and that the other three figures, angel included, are suppliants to the shrine which was the subject of the Gracechurch miracle. If the angel originally bore an Annunciation scroll, it would announce the grace which characterises the Virgin: Ipswich's Blessed Virgin Mary was particularly Our Lady of Grace.

Here, then, is a composition which strongly suggests the events of 1516-1522 at Gracechurch. Above the stem, so redolent of the chief clergy associated with the shrine, together with a young maid and an angel who announces grace, the bowl panels are a joyous Marian composition in the presence of the monarch and his devout consort. It is not likely that a shrine church such as Gracechurch would itself have possessed a font, which would normally be the prerogative of the parish church in whose parish the shrine lay. By contrast St Matthew's parish church was Dr Bailey's church, the place where he planned to be buried, and it would be perfectly natural for him thus to commemorate by a new font the most exciting, dramatic and satisfying event of his life: an exultant statement of confidence in the shrine for which he had achieved so much.

One other possibility for clerical patronage seems unlikely: this font does not look like a gift from Cardinal Thomas Wolsey. Every object commissioned by Wolsey anywhere is infested by cardinals' hats, his heraldry or his personal badge, and here there is the most modest possible presence of the Cardinal, ranged on the lower part of the font alongside a fellow-priest, without any hint of Wolsey's exalted status. Wolsey would not have approved of that. The font has no element of any sort of heraldry, apart from symbols of monarchy, and while Wolsey had become armigerous, Dr Bailey remained without coat-armour. The most likely inspiration for this ambitious addition to St Matthew's church is therefore its rector.

If the font was commissioned in the early 1520s, the presence of both Wolsey and Bailey on the stem would be ironic, for it was donated amid a growing struggle around the future of Gracechurch between Thomas Wolsey and John Bailey. Perhaps one could read the gesture of the two apposed clerical figures as conciliatory on Bailey's part, but it might also be seen a subtle gesture of defiance against the Cardinal, whose designs on the shrine were becoming clear as his plans for a permanent memorial to himself unfolded through the decade.

Two clerics clash: Wolsey and Bailey

Wolsey's triumphal return to Gracechurch on his East Anglian progress of 1517 may have inspired his plans for twin collegiate foundations in Ipswich and Oxford, that at Ipswich being a feeder school for Cardinal College Oxford, in the manner of Eton and King's College, Cambridge. The first formal evidence of the foundations comes from the papal bull of 1524 authorising the suppression of St Frideswide's Priory Oxford to provide the site and revenues for the Oxford College, but Gracechurch had been in Wolsey's mind before that.[72] As early as summer 1521, Wolsey was intent on obtaining a papal bull for an indulgence for Our Lady of Ipswich; on 7 October 1521 his servant John Clerk reassured him from Rome that the bull of indulgence had just been despatched in good form.[73] It must already have been in Wolsey's thoughts that a projected College at Ipswich would be intimately associated with the shrine, and when his new institution eventually emerged in formal shape, it was dedicated to Our Lady. It would be imperative for Wolsey to obtain full control over Gracechurch, which would entail him in also gaining possession of St Matthew's church and parish.

Now Dr Bailey was becoming an obstacle to Wolsey's plans. As we have seen, he might have owed his appointment as Rector to Wolsey in earlier days, but his investment in St Matthew's and Gracechurch had become very personal, and he would not give it up without a fight. The late seventeenth-century antiquary Sir Richard Gipps, when commenting on Bailey's gravestone in the chancel of the church, commented that the Rector had 'contested with Cardinal Wolsey about the alienation of the Great Tithes worth £200.00'.[74] Fortunately for Wolsey, Dr Bailey died in summer 1525. His will, made on 8 July, was given probate in London on 9 September in a slightly confused fashion which suggests that it had been made in a hurry and perhaps with elements of contention: the executors, a couple of Cambridge dons paired with Bailey's senior servant and a veteran town bailiff, with the rising legal star Humphrey Wingfield as their supervisor, all renounced the will before the court regranted it to them as an intestacy.[75] The will includes Bailey's bequest of a bowl to the guild of St Erasmus in the church, but says nothing about the font, and it is also notable that there is no bequest to Gracechurch. All that suggests that Dr Bailey had attended to these important matters in his lifetime, as well as the alternative possibility that the Lord Chancellor of England or the papal *Legatus a latere* (they being one and the same person) had been responsible for some interference in the testamentary process.

There is an interesting timelag between the two formal foundations of Cardinal College, Oxford and Cardinal College, Ipswich. Oxford's was all completed with royal letters patent in May 1526, but at the same time, the English royal representatives in Rome Bishop Jerome Ghinucci and Sir Gregory Casale were only just writing to Wolsey from Rome enclosing the

It is unsurprising that **Thomas Wolsey** inherited no right of bearing arms from his butcher and tavern-keeper father Robert. His uncle Edmund seems to have been the first armigerous member of the Daundy family; if so his sister Joan, Wolsey's mother, would not have been entitled to use them.

When in 1514, Wolsey became archbishop of York and Pope Leo X made him a cardinal, it was *de rigeur* that he should apply for a grant. Sir Thomas Wriothesley was currently Garter King at Arms and it was to him that Wolsey went. In the College of Arms there is a document in Wolsey's hand asking for particulars of the arms of several cardinals and leading churchmen. He was starting from scratch and would put together something to outdo them all by composing an adequately impressive coat for himself and have it granted.

He gave the shield a chief on which were two black Cornish choughs on a gold ground from the arms of St Thomas Becket, his namesake and advower, and in the centre a Tudor Rose to show his closeness and loyalty to King Henry VIII. In base, occupying rather more than half of the shield, by using the correct tinctures he appropriated the arms of both the Ufford earls of Suffolk (the silver cross engrailed on a black ground) and added four blue leopards' faces from the coat of the Delapoles, earls and dukes of Suffolk. The red lion passant at the centre of the cross was a tribute to Pope Leo X. The griffin supporters each held one of the silver pillars always carried before Wolsey in procession, and as a cardinal his hat and tassels took the place of a crest.

As **Thomas Winter** was Wolsey's son by his mistress Joan Lark, he could have used his father's coat by the addition of one of the standard marks of bastardy, but that would have been indiscreet. The herald who granted Joan Lark of Thetford arms (or his clerk) must have enjoyed adding that her grant was made 'because she was very virtuous'. (College of Arms: Misc grants II/113).

It was better to start afresh when in 1526 the 15 year-old, far too young for ordination, held the deanery of Wells, and needed arms; again Wolsey went to Wriothesley for a grant. He chose the same layout as on his own shield, a cross in base and a chief with three charges. The cross was plain, red on silver, patriotic for a young Englishman. Four Cornish choughs were made blue, but Winter was after all another Thomas. The leopards' faces were not blue, to lessen the allusion to Delapole, but they stood on a blue chief. The rest of the composition seemed aimed at predicting prosperity for a son who would almost certainly outlive his father and have to stand on his own feet. A gold garb or wheatsheaf occupied the base point, surrounded by bezants, gold coins, and the leopards' faces and lion rampant on the chief were made gold also. The crest was set on a silver and black wreath and used the upper half of one of Wolsey's supporter griffins, red, with its wings divided vertically gold and blue. There was a coronet around the griffin's neck and in its dexter claw it grasped a gold wheatsheaf.

Soon, young Winter was in Paris, squandering the £300 a year his father allowed him from the stipends of his growing number of sinecures. From 1530 he would need all the gold omens on his arms.

Pope's bulls for Ipswich.[76] The paperwork from the Crown for the Ipswich College was yet to be done, and in fact it took until 1528 to get Cardinal College Ipswich fully founded in the same fashion as Oxford. There were legal complications about Ipswich's endowment, which Thomas Cromwell wearily described to another of Wolsey's servants on 30 June 1528, but this does not account for the time-lag between the two foundations at Oxford and Ipswich.[77]

The most likely reason for the delay at Ipswich in 1525-26 was the problem presented by John Bailey. To avoid any further trouble from independent-minded clergy, Wolsey made the most bizarre appointment possible to St Matthew's and Gracechurch as a successor to Dr Bailey: his own bastard son Thomas Winter, who would have been about fifteen when Bailey died in 1525. When on 26 March 1526 Winter was granted a coat of arms (coincidentally much resembling that of Wolsey in layout), he was already named, amid much else including the Deanery of Wells Cathedral, as Rector of St Matthew's. By 12 November 1526, Winter was also Archdeacon of Suffolk, thanks to the pliancy of the previous Archdeacon in resigning.[78] Wolsey's chaplain Dr Cuthbert Marshall was involved in a presumably technical legal transaction over the Archdeaconry and St Matthew's with Gracechurch, 'resigning' these

benefices to Winter by a notarial instrument of 1 December 1528 in return for equivalent preferment. This was no doubt to fortify a transaction which, by the reasonably high standards of the late medieval English Church, was dubious in the extreme; it was much worse than a return to the pluralist days of Robert Booth and Edmund Assheton for the parish of St Matthew.[79]

The reaction of traditional churchmen and prominent laity in Suffolk to all this was not favourable, although for the moment they would have to hold their tongues.[80] Now the Cardinal could do what he liked, as he happily moved to create the most lavish educational institution ever proposed in Suffolk. On 26 June 1528 he obtained a royal grant of the perpetual advowson of St Matthew's, with the power to unite it to his College of St Mary.[81] He may actually have had thoughts about physically siting his new College at Gracechurch, since only three days after this grant, he was given licence to found a college in the parish of St Matthew or in any convenient place in the town.[82] By then, nevertheless, the Cardinal was presumably just keeping his options open for future expansion of the collegiate ensemble, for his choice of site was already well settled on the priory of St Peter which he had recently dissolved on his legatine authority, and whose future was dealt with in the same batch of paperwork.[83] Perhaps Wolsey respected the presence of the almshouses refounded by his uncle Edmund Daundy beside Gracechurch; no doubt they could also have gained a lavish upgrade if the Cardinal and his schemes had endured longer. Yet any such scruples did not apply to another part of the Cardinal's plans for his new foundation: in a move which illustrates why he became so unpopular with natural supporters of traditional religion, he proposed to annex for his own use the very house where Lord Curson had entertained the Maid of Ipswich during the wonders of 1516. Lord Curson's letter to the Cardinal in the summer of 1529, unhappily begging for compensatory lands and also for three years' grace while he found another house, makes sad reading.[84]

On 26 September 1528 the first Dean of Cardinal College Ipswich, Dr William Capon, wrote to Cardinal Wolsey proudly describing the opening ceremonies of the College which had been held around the appropriate feast of the Nativity of the Blessed Virgin (8 September); this was intended to continue in perpetuity as the College's special festival.[85] The prominence of Gracechurch in the ceremonies will not by now surprise the reader; on the eve of the feast (7 September), the whole College company sang a first evensong in their own chapel, the former parish and priory church of St Peter, which Wolsey was radically modifying for their use. Then everyone processed down to the shrine chapel for evensong there, accompanied by Wolsey's servants Edward Lee, Thomas Cromwell and Stephen Gardiner, plus the town Bailiffs and portmen and the prior of Holy Trinity. The next day would have taken the same pattern, but torrential rain meant that St Peter's alone had to do, with this time further augmentations of local county worthies, in a similar fashion to the crowd which had witnessed the Maid of Ipswich's convulsions twelve years before. One of them, the now-indispensable worthy in any great Ipswich occasion, was the supervisor of Dr Bailey's will, Humphrey Wingfield, 'to whom all we of your graces college byn moche boundyn unto for his loving and kynde maner shewed unto us', Capon said unctuously. Sir Thomas Wentworth of Nettlestead, soon to be Lord Wentworth, was there heading the list of the county gentry, but a notable absentee was Lord Curson, no doubt already apprised of the Cardinal's plans to make him homeless.[86]

The new and modishly classical College seal of Cardinal College Ipswich depicted an image of Mary, which in a remarkable way combines the elements of two panels on the font at St Matthew's, the Coronation and Assumption of the Virgin. Comparable with the Assumption panel is the fact that Mary is standing

Seal of Cardinal College 1528.

against a radiate background within a mandorla and flanked by angels: the main difference is that on the seal, Mary is depicted exposing on her breast a heart surmounted by a cross, rather than praying, and is also standing on a crescent moon. From the Coronation panel on the font come the crowned

Just as the seal combines Assumption and Coronation, the woodcut illustrating the hermit Richard Rolle's *Remedy against temptations* (1508), has the Virgin rising already crowned and bearing the infant Christ. Correct are the rayed mandorla set in clouds and the moon at Mary's feet.

figures of the Father and Son with the Holy Spirit in the form of a dove, which are placed on the seal above the mandorla, though their crowns are much more elongated and surmounted by crosses. We need not think that the designer of the seal had seen the font at

St Matthew's; his design was the most sophisticated of Renaissance work, while the slightly barbarous magnificence of the font was entirely late Gothic – but he may well have had the design of the font panels described to him, and then been told to amalgamate their motifs.[87]

In fact, if Dean Capon had known, Wolsey's vast edifice of extravagance and interlinked power was already crumbling, and soon all the great plans for Cardinal College Ipswich were thrown into reverse. By the end of 1530, its remaining personnel had been sent packing to whatever jobs they might find elsewhere. The shrine of Our Lady of Grace would have to be dealt with, amid the disaster. In fact for the time being, with traditional devotion not officially under attack, it was safe. On 27 September 1532, after what must have been three very anxious years at Gracechurch, the shrine was granted along with a tranche of other former College properties to the Dean and Canons of St George's Chapel, Windsor, together with the Rectory of St Matthew's and the tithes for which Dr Bailey had fought so hard against Wolsey.[88] The good old Rector would have approved, and there surely could be no safer guardian of Gracechurch than the King's private chapel, with its cult of Henry VI flourishing amid many other traditional delights for the pilgrim.

Perhaps the old devotional life could indeed continue. In 1536 comes the last casual topographical reference to the shrine in a legal transaction, when the town bailiffs Robert Bray and John Pypho leased a small piece of land which lay on the road north from the chapel, for it was described as abutting on the south on the upper part of the town ditch and on the north 'on the common way from Holy Trinity [Christ Church] Priory to St Mary's chapel called Our Lady of Grace'.[89] The beautiful Marian font in St Matthew's church was still esteemed by leading parishioners: one of them, William Barker, cooper, made his will that same year 12 August 1536.[90] Amid much else that was traditional, including a bequest to St Matthew's parish guild of St Erasmus and money for soul masses in the church, Barker made a legacy for a covering for the font of St Matthew's, to resemble the font cover at neighbouring St Peter's, at whatsoever charge were necessary. That sounds as if he was completing a scheme for the font which was still recent and which he hoped to take the credit for finishing.

In 1824, D.E. Davy saw a font cover in St Matthew's which has not survived, and might have been that provided for by William Barker: 'a large wooden type [cover omitted] comes up which opens with folding doors'.[91] This strongly suggests a similar design to the font cover with ogee dome which

Bramford font cover

remains in place at nearby Bramford parish church, now carefully deprived of all popish figurative imagery on its main panels, but of a latest Gothic style blending into classical detail: the Bramford cover is likewise of the 1530s or 1540s, paralleling Barker's plans for St Matthew's and the lost cover at St Peter's, which no doubt Cardinal Wolsey had commissioned.

The coming of Reformation: destruction

These were nevertheless not safe times for traditional religion anywhere in the realm. Whatever one's assessment of the Maid of Ipswich's dramatic performances in 1516, it has to be said that the girl was being remarkably prescient in exhorting her audience to be 'steadfast' in traditional faith. She could not have known (at least by any earthly means) that less than eighteen months later, far away in Saxony, Martin Luther was to make his first defiance against the Church authorities. Even while those two very traditional clerics Dr Bailey and Wolsey fought their legal duel in the 1520s, the reverberations of Luther's religious revolution had been reaching Henry VIII's island kingdom. The first signs of trouble for Gracechurch's survival had come in 1527, when the Norfolk-born Cambridge don Thomas Bilney made a spectacular intervention in Ipswich's devotional life with a touring campaign against East Anglian and Home Counties shrines, for which he was put on trial at the end of that year. It was the same year in which William Tyndale first sneered at the Gracechurch miracle in his *Obedience of a Christian Man*. The forces of destruction were gathering.

In the course of a sermon in Holy Trinity (Christ Church) Priory in Ipswich, attacking saintly mediation and pilgrimages, Bilney announced 'that the miracles done at Walsingham and Ca[n]terbury and there in Ipswitch were done by the devill, by the sufferance of God to blind the pore people.' He was speaking a mere eleven years after the Maid had had her visions, on her home territory. It is likely that Bilney made an even more direct defiance against Gracechurch in 1527, almost within earshot of the shrine. John Foxe's transcription of the deposition on the Christ Church sermon in the 1563 edition of his *Acts and Monuments* was accompanied by an illustration of the preacher being pulled from a pulpit against a labelled background picture of the church of St George, Ipswich, which as we have seen, stood virtually across the road from Gracechurch. The picture is no doubt meant to convey that this was the scene of the sermon which caused his ejection from the pulpit (it was one of two such ejections in the diocese of Norwich, the deposition tells us).[92]

Bilney's denunciations made a great impression locally, and now there were plenty to echo his sentiments, even from his fellow-clergy in the pulpit. In northern Essex, amid a mass of depositions taken from a large network of Essex and Suffolk Lollards detected and examined by the London diocesan court in summer 1528, there is the testimony of John Pykas of St Nicholas's parish, Colchester, who defiantly told Bishop Tunstall of London that he had heard 'Mr

Thomas Bilney woodcut from Foxe showing St George's with a round west tower.

Bylney and other preachers at Ipswich say that it was but folly to go on pilgrimages', and that Bilney's sermon was 'most ghostly' [i.e. spiritually-inspired]. Pykas specifically said that he spread these opinions after he had heard them preached.[93] Another deponent also testified that he had heard Pykas opine at much the same time that it was 'mysavory' [misguided] to go on pilgrimages to Walsingham, Ipswich or elsewhere, for it was idolatry.[94] Besides this, we have the words of Richard Fox, radically-minded parish priest of Steeple Bumpstead in north Essex: sometime around Christmas 1527: he sneered at the traditionalist devotion of one of his parishioners, John Darkyns, saying 'Ye make a vow or a behest to go in pilgrimage to Our Lady of Ipswich, Walsingham, or to Canterbury, and there by a candle of wax think ye do well.' Challenged by Darkyns to affirm the practice, Fox remained silent – but it is significant that he had named exactly the same trio of shrines which Bilney had denounced a few months earlier.[95]

And so the diocesan lawyers gloomily catalogued a growing pile of insults to Our Lady of Ipswich and her companions. Thomas Bowgas of St Leonard's Colchester chose to make a similar observation to Richard Fox's in relation to Canterbury or Ipswich, adding his wish to burn the Ipswich image: 'I would Our Lady of Grace were in my bakehouse [backhouse]' – with the alternative of throwing it with a range of other holy images into the sea from a ship.[96] Henry Raylond of Colchester denied calling Our Lady of Ipswich an idol, but he probably did.[97] That does not exhaust the welter of references to Gracechurch in these depositions. Clearly it was a major object of loathing within the local groups of Essex and Suffolk Lollards who, thanks to Bilney and his fellow-activists, were now merging their century-and-a-half of image-

hatred with the new message of evangelical reformers. Small wonder that a (reasonably light) penance which an unnamed member of the group received from the Bishop of London's court in October 1528 included the offering of a candle weighing a pound to the image of Our Lady, and an order to visit 'the Abbey of Ipswich' (*abbatiam de Ipiswico* – Holy Trinity, presumably) on Our Lady's feast of the Purification, reciting seven penitential psalms and five Lady Psalters.[98]

By 1529, Sir Thomas More felt it an urgent necessity to defend traditional religion against such increasingly open attacks, which he did at huge length in his *Dialogue concerning Heresies*, already cited. In the section of his text which turned to Ipswich, he proceeded from his championing of Mistress Wentworth to use Gracechurch as a means of presenting and pre-empting one Protestant argument against devotion to the saints. It was a theme which needed careful treatment because of the plausibility of its critical observation of traditional religion:

> they wyll make comparysons betwene our lady of Ipswych and our lady of walsyngam / As weenyng the one ymage more of power then the tother / whych they wold neuer doo / but if instede of our lady they put theyre truste in the Image selfe. And the people in spekyng of our lady / Of all our ladyes sayeth one / I loue beste our lady of walsingham / And I sayth the other oure lady of Ipeswyche. In

whyche wordys what menyth she but her loue and her affeccyon to the stok [lump of wood] that standyth in the chapell at walsyngham or Ipswych.[99]

More echoed this standard Protestant theme about images solely in order to knock it down in extended fashion, but there were many who would have been happy to accept the argument, including William Tyndale, who the following year, made a spirited reply to More's defence of the Wentworth miracle in his *Answer to Sir Thomas More's Dialogue*.[100] Soon afterwards Thomas Bilney was destroyed for his beliefs, burned at the stake in Norwich in 1531, but his death only inflamed the passions of his East Anglian devotees. During 1531 and 1532 a campaign of popular violence broke in south Suffolk and north Essex which can be considered to be evangelical revenge for Bilney's martyrdom; the victims were not human, but those local cult objects which were vulnerable because they were in the open air or not well-guarded. Among them were a crucifix 'of Saint Mary the Virgin of Ipswich' (*Sanctae Mariae Virginis Gipwici*), which is most likely to have been the wayside cross beside the shrine church itself; another victim was the Good Rood of Dovercourt, the object of Abbot Reve's pilgrimage vow in the wake of the Maid's recovery.[101] This seems very targeted iconoclasm with Our Lady of Ipswich in mind. It is stark confirmation of the rage which we have heard expressed in 1528 against the Ipswich devotion, in the London diocesan court depositions of Essex and Suffolk Lollards and evangelicals, from precisely the same area in which the violence was taking place.

Although the wayside cross by Our Lady's shrine was damaged in 1531, it was repaired, for there are references to this cross in St Matthew's Street well into the seventeenth century, under the name of the 'Stoning Cross'; whatever its popish origins, it was a useful waymark, employed for instance in 1604 as a stopping-point for the examination of travellers into town in a time of plague.[102] It is depicted still surviving in the topographical panorama of Ipswich in 1600, which forms the background of the painted wooden memorial plaque in St Mary-le-Tower church to a rather conservative-minded Ipswich worthy, William Smarte, and his wife. The small illustration is nevertheless a witness to the changed times in Ipswich, as in it the 'cross' appears as no more than a plain obelisk: no crucifix would have been acceptable in public in late Elizabethan Ipswich at the end of half a century of relentless Reformation. The shrine itself was quickly menaced by an even more dangerous foe than local East Anglian activists, and a man very well known to Thomas More: Cardinal Wolsey's former servant Thomas Cromwell.

This excerpt from the memorial to William and Alice Smarte (oil on board, mural in St Mary-le-Tower) shows the left hand (west) end of the earliest known panoramic view of Ipswich. St Matthew's church nestles beneath her right arm, and a tall stone cross welcomes visitors on their way from Bury or Norwich to the Shrine of Our Lady of Grace. Directly beneath it is Handford Mill with its waterwheel prominent. In front of Alice level with her waist can be seen the Westgate, with Lady Lane running down and the road to St George's chapel rising up past some fine houses.

Besides his very considerable dose of political ruthlessness, Cromwell possessed a sympathy for the Reformation which was turning into a discreet but radical determination to destroy the entire world of English traditional devotion, in a manner which would have delighted the now-martyred Bilney, and which would fulfil the destructive hopes of Thomas Bowgas. Cromwell's career very quickly recovered from the disaster of Wolsey's fall and put him in a position to achieve his aims. Within three years of entering royal service in 1531, he was not just Principal Secretary and the most powerful figure in royal administration; he gained the offices first of Vicar-General, then of Vice-Gerent in Spirituals. This 'Vice-Gerency' was a brand-new title which concealed the fact that he had reconstructed precisely the powers in the Church that his old master Wolsey had held, although now exercised on behalf of the King rather than the Pope.

As the former chief legal deviser of Cardinal College, Ipswich, Cromwell had good cause to remember the damp two days he had spent in the vicinity of the shrine of Our Lady of Ipswich at the inauguration of the College back in 1528, and as Wolsey's old servant, he would have been well aware of Bilney's diatribes in 1527 against the miracle of Ipswich. Moreover, in his capacity as royal Secretary and Vice-Gerent, he continued to have close contacts with Ipswich, and he continued to take a direct interest in the revenues of Gracechurch, despite its nominal custodianship by the Dean and Canons of Windsor. In June 1534, a couple of months after Elizabeth Barton had been executed, Cromwell commissioned his old friend Sir Thomas Rush (sheriff of Suffolk that year, and also a close associate of Lord Curson) to visit Gracechurch. This revealed that the shrine, now so controversial and so physically beleaguered, was already struggling.[103]

Rush reported to Cromwell that he had taken a reckoning from the shrine's keeper for wax candles and other souvenir images, 'which was never soo lityll. Devocion is decayde, as doth a pere by the same, as your servant William Lawrence shall declare [to you]'. Lawrence, as we will see, was to persist in his careful scrutiny of the shrine's business, until there was no longer any business to transact. Rush's report makes it evident that the atmosphere was changing in Ipswich, which must have relieved Thomas Cromwell mightily: there was not going to be any flourishing Marian cult at the Ipswich shrine to echo the political dangers which Elizabeth Barton had lately represented for King Henry's regime. Cardinal Wolsey's ignominious fall so soon after his energetic efforts to associate himself so closely with

Gracechurch cannot have been good for the shrine's prestige, either nationally or locally. Even apart from the enflaming effect of Thomas Bilney's death in East Anglia, the momentous religious changes in the kingdom which followed Henry's break with the Pope in 1533 were beginning to affect the devotional habits of ordinary people throughout the realm; Ipswich and its surrounding countryside were rapidly emerging as one of England's most precocious centres of Protestantism.

By 1536 the destructive direction of government religious policy was becoming plain, and it deeply disturbed many of conservative outlook. One of them was an Essex-based former Cambridge don, Dr Robert Crewkhorne (Crewkerne?), who had more than one connection with the shrine of our Lady of Grace. In his younger days he had been a younger colleague of Dr John Bailey as a Fellow of Pembroke Hall, Cambridge, but he was now resident at Wivenhoe in Essex as almoner to Elizabeth de Vere (née Beaumont), Dowager Countess of Oxford. She was a lady magnificently traditional in her religion, whose sister at Barking Abbey and niece at the London Minories would have been able to tell her much about the Maid of Kent and the other Wentworth sisters; moreover, one of her favourite maids, Katherine Christmas, was the daughter of a prominent former servant of that devout pilgrim to Our Lady of Grace Queen Katherine of Aragon.[104]

The turbulent evangelicalism in the territory around Wivenhoe between Colchester and Ipswich had evidently put Crewkhorne under severe emotional strain, and in late February 1536 Thomas Dorset, a London priest, reported to friends in Plymouth that he had witnessed Dr Crewkhorne's examination at Lambeth Palace before Archbishop Cranmer and two other leading evangelical bishops about his prophetic visions. Crewkhorne was telling this deeply unsympathetic audience that he had been rapt into Heaven, to behold not only the Trinity (three bodies with two legs between them, apparently), but also our Lady, who took him by the hand 'and bad him serve her as he had doon in tyme passed, and bad hym to preche aborde [abroad] that she wold be honorid at Eppiswhiche and at Willisdon as she hath bee[n] in old tymes'.[105] Those times were clearly past, in Crewkhorne's mind at least: this confirms the impression given by Sir Thomas Rush in 1534 that already the Ipswich cult was in a state of steep decline.

Dr Crewkhorne's distress was understandable. He may well have known of an ominous new publication, dating from a few months before Dorset's letter. In 1535 a printer close to Vice-Gerent Cromwell, William Marshall, published the first semi-official Tudor attack on the world of images and shrines. It was actually a translation of a German original by Martin Bucer, leading pastor of the influential Protestant city of Strassburg, although the English reader was not informed of this incendiary origin. Obviously a *succès de scandale,* it went through two editions, the second of which answered criticisms from infuriated traditionalists, and added a little more local colour to suit the English market in the form of new marginal notes. Among these was the menacing thought 'Wolde god the miracles of the ymagis of Walsyngham, Cantorbury, Yppeswiche, Hayles, Worcester, and Chestre, and suche other wer well tryed bi scripture to see what article of our faith they have confirmed.'[106] In this contemptuous round-up of half a dozen prime English shrines, it is noticeable that half of them were wonder-working images of Our Lady: Walsingham, Ipswich and Worcester. A note to the text elsewhere anticipated their fate: 'The bokes of the hevenly worde of god have ben brente [burned], and blynde ymages have ben set up in their stede, but now we trust our bright bokes shall be restored to us and these blind bokes shall be brent'.[107]

And so precisely it fell out: bibles came in, and images were ousted, on bonfires. Beginning in 1536, soon after Dr Crewkhorne had been humiliated at the hands of Cranmer and his like-minded episcopal colleagues, Cromwell saw to the distribution of the first officially-sanctioned English Bible since Anglo-Saxon times, and two years later, he turned his attention to his campaign of destruction of shrines, among which Ipswich was among the earliest victims. The sequence began with the Rood in Boxley Abbey in Kent in February 1538, burned in a spectacular and mocking public demonstration in London on 24 February. The destruction of the shrine of St Edmund at Bury, from whence Abbot Reve had set out to see the Maid of Ipswich back in the very different days of 1516, was part of the same campaign that month.[108] 1538 proved a great year for burnings in very contrasting ways: on one side, the deaths of the evangelical John Lambert and various unfortunate Anabaptist immigrants, proving Henry VIII's grotesque version of the 'middle way' by balancing the fiery destruction of symbols of traditional religion. On the opposite and traditionalist side, there was the Welsh equestrian statue of Derfel Gadarn, gruesomely used to fuel the fire which burned Friar John Forest, Katherine of Aragon's former partisan and defender of traditional religion, on 22 May. Thomas Becket's shrine at Canterbury was to follow into oblivion in September 1538, perhaps with deliberate irony, on the feast of the Nativity of the Blessed Virgin Mary, and it was also around that time that the final end came for a host of shrine images, including Our Ladies of Ipswich and Walsingham.[109]

From early in 1538, the devotional life of Gracechurch, already significantly struggling in 1534, as Sir Thomas Rush had observed, was being stifled out of existence. Cromwell's ecclesiastical visitors reached Ipswich in April 1538, to intimidate the Franciscan friary (Greyfriars) into closure with the aid of the friars' unsympathetic hereditary patron, none other than Thomas Lord Wentworth. Greyfriars was the closest of Ipswich's three friaries to Gracechurch. Cromwell's local agent William Lawrence reported the visitors' doings in April, along with what he himself was now doing to minimise the devotional life at Our Lady's shrine. He had deprived the shrine of its goods apart from a chalice and two vestments, and he wanted to know what to do with the money in the chapel chest, particularly if the chapel clerk was to be discharged, and how he should deal with Sir Roger Wentworth's two priests still singing there.[110] If this William Lawrence is the same as the Ipswich weaver who made his will on 14 May 1538 and who was dead by the date of its probate on 14 August that same year, his bequests in the will for soul prayers and reparations for his parish church of St Nicholas show no signs of evangelical zeal, but he knew what his master Cromwell would want to happen.[111]

The subsequent removal of the image of Our Lady of Ipswich is very well documented. First there is Bishop Latimer's nudge to Cromwell to round up pilgrimage images of the Virgin nationwide, in a letter of 21 June 1538, a plan which they had no doubt already discussed at length.[112] Then we have a letter of William Lawrence to Cromwell from Ipswich, telling of his co-operation with Lord Wentworth in removing the image with such discretion 'that shee was conveyed in to the Shipp that very fewe ware prevy to yt, and shall cum upp [to London] so shortly as the wynd will serve.'[113] This cannot have been long before the letter of Thomas Thacker to Cromwell on 30 July, saying that Lawrence had sent him the image, which (thanks to a Protestant wind?) was now safe in Cromwell's mansion at the Austin Friars in London, awaiting his Lordship's pleasure. 'Ther is nothing about hir but ij. half shoes of silver, and iiij. stones of cristall sett in silver', he remarked scrupulously, or dismissively.[114] She still there on 1 September, when Thacker told his master that he had stacked up the 'bare Imagis' of our Lady of Buxton and St Modwenna of Burton-on Trent next to her, victims of a new Protestant forage through the Midlands.[115]

The next that we know, without an exact date, is the chronicler Charles Wriothesley's note that the images of Our Ladies of Walsingham and Ipswich and many others from across England and Wales, which had been gathered together in London during July, 'were burnt at Chelsey by my Lord Privie Seale' (that is, Cromwell).[116] It is not unlikely that this fiery demonstration at Chelsea was timed to coincide with the destruction of Thomas Becket's shrine and his public denunciation as a traitor to Henry II, in the first two weeks of September 1538. Thomas Lord Wentworth would have remembered his attendance at the grand dedication ceremonies at Cardinal College and Gracechurch only a decade before, but that had been in a very different world; and firm and energetic evangelical that he was, he would have been pleased at the transformation. All this activity gave him the chance now to engineer a radical shift in power towards the evangelical party in the borough of Ipswich, which at root was never going to be reversed in the Tudor or early Stuart periods.[117]

Wentworth's client John Bale, who was beneficed in Suffolk at the time, expressed his rejoicing in a pruriently comic play *Three Laws*, published possibly in 1548, but clearly written much earlier, at this moment of transformation in the late 1530s. The villainous, hypocritical and pleasure-loving figure of 'Infidelity', that is, traditional religion, is involved in an argument with 'The Law of Moses' (standing in for good evangelical faith). Infidelity laments the lost world of shrines, pilgrimages and the stories of the saints. He ranges Gracechurch alongside St Edmund's shrine at Bury and the Holy Blood relic at Hailes in Gloucestershire – all three of them were destroyed during 1538, which makes it almost certain that Bale's play can be dated quite precisely to the last few months of that year:

> It was a good world, whan we had soch wholsom storyes
> Preached in our churche, on sondayes & other feryes [feria days].
> With us was it merye,
> Whan we went to Berye.
> And to our lady of grace,
> To the bloude of hayles,
> Where no good chere fayles,
> And other holye place.

There can be little doubt that this aggressive piece of Cromwellian propaganda saw some performances in Ipswich during autumn 1538.[119]

As far as Cromwell was concerned, there only remained the matter of gathering in cash from the sale of items from the shrine chapel: in January 1539 his accounts record the substantial sum of £21.19s 7d received for 'stuff of Our Lady Chapel in Gypwich' sold by William Lawrence. In December 1539, there followed 40s for a chalice also sold by Lawrence –

maybe that was the one chalice which Lawrence had left them at his first visit of confiscation.[120] The Daundy almshouses beside the chapel could now rejoice in their good fortune in having no formal legal connection with the shrine or with Edmund Daundy's chantry at St Lawrence; they survived all the confiscations of chantry property in mid-century, and their foundation, in origins as old as the fourteenth century, still exists for its charitable purpose.

And after the tale of ruthless and ideologically-motivated destruction of the cult of Our Lady which we have reconstructed, it is only fair to put a more positive case, and record that Thomas Cromwell, showing the priorities of a genuinely zealous evangelical, unravelled Cardinal Wolsey's appropriations of the borough school and a parish church. His actions benefitted the townspeople in general and the parishioners of St Peter's church in particular, after they had seen the church and school absorbed into Cardinal College and the church building drastically modified for College use. As far as the restoration of the present Ipswich School was concerned, we know of its formal reconstitution through Queen Elizabeth I's charter of 1565; this confirmed a lost regrant of corporate status from Henry VIII which had also involved the return of old revenues to the foundation.[121]

Cromwell's part in securing this restoration is attested by letter of thanks to him from the town's two bailiffs for 1539-40, William Sabyn and William Nottingham, written on 20 March 1540: they reminded the Lord Privy Seal of his previous goodness to the town in securing the continuance of the common school, and they recommended as its next Master Richard Argentine. Argentine was a respectable scholar who at this stage in his (later notorious) career was playing the Protestant humanist to perfection, to suit the evangelical tone of the borough leadership with his thoroughgoing lectures on Paul's Epistle to the Romans – an anticipation of the town lecturers who would be instituted in the reign of Elizabeth. All this would have been music to Cromwell's ears, and neither writers nor recipient would know that the Lord Privy Seal's political career was about to be abruptly terminated by his own execution.[122]

Cardinal College's closure in 1529/30 had left St. Peter's parish in limbo. By 1538 the church fabric was decaying, virtually all the plate and ornaments had been dispersed, the parishioners were still exiled, half each at St Nicholas and St Mary Quay, and the church itself was redundant. With William Lawrence close at hand in spring 1538 harassing the Ipswich Franciscans into surrender and clearly also preparing for the closure of Gracechurch, a consortium of inhabitants in

Woodcut from Foxe showing many images being carried away for destruction in the reign of Edward VI.

the former parish sought to avoid complete disaster by appealing both to Lawrence and also in a formal petition to Cromwell himself for help to recover the church goods and some parish revenues, and to order all parishioners to come back to St. Peter's for services once more. The survival of the parish into the twentieth century testifies to the success of their rescue operation, and to the strength of their sense of parish pride and identity; but it is clear also that Cromwell and Lawrence paid careful attention to their grievances and helped them in their efforts.[123]

Aftermath: myths and survivals

In relatively modern times, a legend has grown up that Our Lady of Ipswich was saved from the fire at Chelsea by English sailors, who took refuge during a Mediterranean voyage in the small Italian coastal town of Nettuno and donated it to the people there.[124] There is indeed a wooden image of late medieval vintage in Nettuno, but the chances of it being the real Gracechurch image are extremely small. To begin with, it is far too late in character: it hardly fits an image unearthed in the 1320s which would already have been considered of some antiquity when originally discovered. Even more cogently, everyone involved in the removal and destruction of the image, from Thomas Cromwell downwards, personally knew Our Lady of Ipswich very well, and they had every reason to see her completely destroyed.

Maybe an image did really come from Ipswich to Nettuno during the decades of iconoclasm which followed the destruction of Gracechurch – that would not have been difficult or surprising – and maybe confusion arose around what exactly the original nature of it had been. If there really had been an Ipswich connection, it would have been natural and understandable to enhance the image's status with reference to the well-known statue formerly at Gracechurch. Although the legend has lately been a fruitful and pleasant source of exchange visits between Ipswich and Nettuno, and has also recently inspired commendable local ecumenical goodwill in Ipswich, it can be safely dismissed.

By contrast, it is likely that everyone has overlooked a genuine physical survival of the demolished chapel of Gracechurch, reused in the fabric of St Nicholas parish church nearby. Since the eighteenth century, there has been much antiquarian interest in an exceptional collection of Romanesque sculptures incorporated in the fabric at the west end of the south aisle of St Nicholas. Scattered amid unmistakeably later medieval sculpted fragments of window voussoirs and the like, they do not seem all exactly contemporary, but represent an extensive and rich cumulative scheme of iconography produced over a fairly short period, post-Norman Conquest into the twelfth century.[125] Some of the sculpture has in modern times been placed inside the church of St Nicholas (which is now redundant), and among these pieces is a door-tympanum depicting a boar feeding, within a semi-circular arched band. The band bears an inscription, possibly secondary but still twelfth-century in character,

'INDEDI:CATIO[N]E:E[CCL]E[SIE]:OM[NIVM: SANCT]O[R[V]M'.

The Boar tympanum from All Saints, and its reverse with a dedication cross.

We know from the account of D.E. Davy, made at his visit on 30 June 1824, that this and another sculpture of St Michael and the dragon were then still outside, visible high up in the west wall of the south aisle. Both stones had been noticed there by the parson antiquary Richard Canning who was revising the late John Kirby's *Suffolk Traveller* (1735) for a second enlarged edition of 1764. It is likely that quite soon after Davy saw them still in the external wall in 1824, both these sculptures were taken down and brought into the church for protection, when a window was inserted in the aisle west wall to light a new gallery.[126]

The importance of the dedication inscription on the Romanesque boar sculpture is that it almost certainly locates the rest of the early Romanesque reused stonework as coming from the church formerly dedicated to All Saints. Hence all the other ashlar fragments in the walling are likely to have the same origin. We have shown above that that church of All Saints became the chapel of Our Lady of Grace. So given that identification, this is demolition material derived from the shrine church. Most of the fabric of St Nicholas has been dated to c. 1300, but these very miscellaneous building materials of flint and reused ashlar at the western end of the south aisle are different in character from the walling in the rest of the church. The south-west corner of the south aisle is a later extension, or a rebuild of decayed fabric.[127]

We can note that if William Lawrence, Cromwell's agent in the downfall of Gracechurch, was indeed the

Rectangular panel showing the archangel Michael fighting with a dragon.

parishioner of St Nicholas who made his will in 1538, there is a good personal link from the one building to the other. It will be recalled that Lawrence obtained £21.19s 7d for 'stuff of Our Lady Chapel in Gypwich', and such a large sum could have included the actual building materials of the chapel itself, sold to the parish of St Nicholas (metalwork like lead roofing or bells would have been reserved for the King's use). Moreover, with a delightful suggestiveness for our hypothesis, Lawrence left in his will more than a token sum, a mark (13s 4d) for repair work which was then going on in St Nicholas. But equally intriguing is the fact that before its removal indoors in the early nineteenth century, the ancient boar sculpture with its dedication to All Saints had not just been used as random rubble, but had been placed in the aisle wall of St Nicholas facing outwards and the right way up, visible in such a position and at such a height that it could be seen from below, but not too closely scrutinised. Davy had said of the other sculpture with its prominent inscription for St Michael that the inscription was 'too high to be made out without assistance', and he did not notice the All Saints dedication inscription at all when he noted the boar stone which bore it. That dedication inscription (written in very clear twelfth-century capitals, comprehensibly legible even to Tudor eyes) was there for those who were aware of it to appreciate, but not for casual inspection by others.

The west end of the south aisle at St Nicholas showing reused stonework. The two sculptures were seen by Davy in 1824 let into the top of the wall, roughly where the two-light window is today.

In 1538, nevertheless, it would not have been the dedication inscription which chiefly mattered, since it would have meant nothing at all to those not aware of the complex history of the shrine church; what would have been of contemporary significance was the striking design contained within it. As the boar's head sculpture had been the tympanum of a doorway, it would have been familiar to all those who had walked through the door, particularly if it had been a much-used entrance to a much-frequented church. For a generation or more, that door-tympanum would still have remained very recognisable from its former context. With our eyes more attuned to style and historical period than were those of Tudor observers, the collection of sculptures at St Nicholas carries another message: its highly unusual quality and elaboration speaks of a lost church which was given an attention and elaborate decoration very rare among East Anglian minor churches of its date. There must have been something special about All Saints Church Ipswich even in its early incarnation: an exceptional sacred character, maybe a shrine. It is not likely to have been a shrine of Our Lady: the lack of Marian reference in any of its surviving sculptural fragments is noticeable. Yet it would not have be surprising that such a richly-ornamented place had contained at least one significant image of Our Lady, perhaps reverently buried at some stage, only to await rediscovery in the fourteenth century, two hundred years before little Mistress Wentworth demanded to return to that sacred site.

The close attention to the fate of the shrine church paid by William Laurence, both one of Cromwell's servants and a parishioner of St Nicholas, would certainly suggest that this reuse of its material as builders' rubble came quite soon after its dissolution – indeed, that it was torn down straight away. That likelihood is made all the stronger by the casual mention of the former site in a Suffolk rental of the great Norfolk family of Townshend, which dates from 1550 at the latest, and may be some years earlier than that. It refers to a copyhold tenement in the occupation of Henry Veer, for which 'the grounde sometyme callyd o'r lady of graces chappell' formed part of the eastern boundary.[128]

Veer's copyhold was a long property which evidently ran north-south immediately behind both the chapel and the western Daundy almshouses, between (to the north) St Matthew's Street the main road out of town, and (to the south) the 'churche waye' from Lady Lane to St Matthew. The tenement is clearly visible on Ogilby's map of 1674, so the bounds described in this manuscript rental once more confirm the site of Gracechurch on the corner of St Matthew's

Street and Lady Lane. The tenement described was the same property which more than two centuries before, had been in the hands of John de Halteby. By at least 1550, the shrine could be regarded just as a piece of ground. And in its place, Protestant inhabitants of Ipswich could look back to Thomas Cromwell and hold him in grateful memory for restoring their school, helping St Peter's parish back into existence, and making available the materials for substantial repairs to St Nicholas's church. They would think it all a fair exchange.

Another act of oblivion surely has more significance than mere accidental destruction: the disappearance of the tomb of Robert, Lord Curson, chronicler of the Maid, after his family had strenuously tried to save his memory and funeral monument amid the dissolutions of 1538. In his will, made on 31 October 1534 and proved the following March, Curson had made elaborate provisions for his burial, which he stipulated should be in the church of the Ipswich Greyfriars; he bequeathed the Franciscans much more money than he did the Whitefriars and Blackfriars.[129] When in April 1538 Cromwell's visitors (including William Laurence) made their inventory of goods at the Greyfriars before dissolving the house, these included 'ij feyer silk pelowys' formerly Lady Curson's (presumably his first wife Anne) and 'a feyn herse clothe that ley upon the lorde Cursons herse'. The second item suggests that the tomb was designed with a metal 'hearse' superstructure, a handful of which can still be seen placed on such sumptuous medieval monuments as that of Earl Richard Beauchamp at St Mary's Warwick or Sir John Marmion at West Tanfield (Yorkshire).[130]

Curson's family then made sure that the tomb housing him and his first wife was taken out of Greyfriars church as the building was being closed in 1538. It was re-erected in another nearby religious building which we have seen much associated with the last years of the shrine, the parish church of St Peter, which had so briefly served as the chapel of Cardinal College. In 1568, Curson's second wife Dame Margaret, now widow of Sir Edward Green (a lady whom we have already met, as the step-mother of the Catholic recusant Rooke Green, executor to the Maid of Ipswich's brother) made her will and requested burial in St Peter's 'by the burial of the saide late lorde Curson and the ladie his first wife'. She had already shown her interest in the church by giving it 13s 4d for repairs in 1566. When she in turn died in 1577, her wishes were carried out, at some considerable and unusual expense revealed in the churchwardens' accounts, which must indicate some substantial modification to the now forty-year-old monument.[131]

Why, then, do we see no trace now in St Peter's Church of this monument, clearly so important and prominent, when there is a profusion of monuments within the church dating from the beginning of the seventeenth century onwards? It has to have disappeared very early after its rebuilding for Dame Margaret Green. There is no early antiquarian account of it, not a scrap even about its heraldic display, when the likes of Henry Chitting, William Hervey, William Tyllotson, John Weever, all of whom have left us some notes on Ipswich churches from before the 1630s, would have been expected to have left us some record.[132] The suspicion arises that in Puritan Ipswich, the monument carried considerable ideological significance from the past, and that reputation cannot have been helped by Dame Margaret Green's modifications to it for her own benefit.

There is no doubt that right into her last years, Dame Margaret shared her son Rooke Green's pronounced religious conservatism, which in his case, met the new dynamism of the Counter-Reformation and flowered into open Catholic recusancy.[133] Neither he nor she would have forgotten the events in Ipswich which had changed the life of Rooke Greene's close friend, Sir John Wentworth of Gosfield, back in 1516. When the twice-widowed *grande dame* made her will in 1568, fourteen years after the death of her second husband, she quite blatantly provided for a traditional requiem mass and funeral dole at St Peter's, within the limits of what was possible in the present Protestant dispensation of the Church of England. She requested 'a communion with the poor, and to every of the poor which shall receive communion 4d and to the minister 12d.' We will never know if that particular bequest was honoured in 1577 when her will was proved, but as the decades went by, it would have been increasingly unlikely, with so many watchful eyes among the borough's Puritan governors.

One obvious opportunity for the removal of the Curson tomb would have been during the very extensive rebuilding works to create a new chancel for the church, which St Peter's churchwardens' accounts reveal as taking place in 1593, alongside major work on the church tower.[134] This chancel project can be seen the last fall-out from Cardinal Wolsey's plans for Cardinal College and the shrine of Our Lady of Ipswich. It was necessary because of Wolsey's demolition of the eastern (monastic) parts of the church, during his conversion of St Peter's to the College chapel; his fall and the College's closure had probably prevented him building a new choir on to the church appropriate to his magnificence, leaving only some hasty improvised work closing off the east end of what remained of the building; the churchwardens had had to deal in 1573 with 'stone that fell down at the chancell end'.[135] There is in fact an intriguing entry in the 1593 building accounts, 'for stoping up of ii graves vˢ'.

Such a prompt removal of the Curson/Green monument would account for the lack of any description of the tomb by Elizabethan and Jacobean antiquaries. There would be no surprise if its disappearance were a last act of revenge by Ipswich's Protestant ascendancy on the symbolic memory of the shrine of Our Lady and its greatest miracle which Dame Margaret Green's first husband Lord Curson had chronicled. Any such destruction would have constituted an extraordinary gesture of contempt towards her son the recusant Rooke Green, who did not die until 1602 – but most telling of all is the fact that when Dame Margaret was buried in the church and fees had to be paid, the churchwardens of St Peter spoke of her executors not as 'My Lady Green's', but '*my Ladye Curssams*'. In 1577, that was reaching back to memories decades old, fraught with present-day meaning.[136]

It is worth noting in this connection that although Our Lady of Ipswich did not slide quickly into oblivion, most open references to her after her shrine's destruction come from her enemies.[137] As we have seen, the sensational exploits of Mistress Wentworth are preserved for us partly through Protestant sneers, from John Bale in 1545 to Cranmer's anonymous editor in 1556. For a generation or two, Gracechurch remained one item in a list of shrines in whose wrecking English Protestants rejoiced. Bale could not leave alone the memory of the shrine which his patron Lord Wentworth had nudged towards destruction. It was interesting that in his 1545 diatribe, Bale went straight on from his sarcastic reminiscence about Dr Bailey's part in the Gracechurch miracle to speak equally scornfully of Elizabeth Barton the Maid of Kent and her clerical patron Dr Edward Bocking, and then on to Dr Crewkhorne, Dr Bailey's old colleague, who as we have seen had wanted to preach in favour of Our Lady of Ipswich in 1536: 'Doctor Cronkeshorne had certen reuelacions of a newe kyngedome that was commynge vpon this clause of Te Deum, *Aperuisti credentibus regna celorum*. And preached them in dyuerse townes of Eastsexe [Essex] as the monasteryes were in suppressynge'.[138] Evidently Bale saw as very closely connected that clerical trio of Suffolk, Kentish and Essex DDs and their ability to deceive ordinary folk (as a Cambridge man, he would have known Bailey and Crewkhorne personally). Probably a couple of years later, in 1547, Bale put into print the script of his play, *Three Laws of Nature, Moses and Christ*, which he had written a decade before, in the aftermath of Cromwell's campaign against pilgrimage in 1538, celebrating in its text the fall of the shrine of Ipswich.

From the same evangelical establishment circle, but at an even more exalted level, came further contemptuous allusions. Archbishop Thomas Cranmer, in no less public a work than a catechism intended to instruct all the children of England, issued in 1548, made reference to Gracechurch in a list of cultic images, all of which had been destroyed in Cromwell's campaign of 1538. He had been speaking of the superstitions associated with the cult of the saints,

> whiche abuses good children, your owne fathers, yf you aske theym, can well declare vnto you. For they themselfes wer greatly seduced by certayne famouse and notoriouse ymages, as by our lady of walsingham, oure ladye of Ippeswiche, Saynt Thomas of Canterbury, Sainct Anne of Buckestone, the roode of Grace, and suche lyke, whom many of your parentes visitide yerely, leauinge their owne houses and familyes.[139]

Cranmer's 1548 catechism was not a success, being an over-hasty adaptation and translation of a Lutheran work whose message no longer suited his theological plans, so it was soon displaced by something even more radically Protestant. Yet Cranmer's circle did not forget Gracechurch, as we have already seen in the Protestant diatribe published in Wesel in 1556 (above, p. 27). And the theme was still repeated in the new Homily against Idolatry in Queen Elizabeth's set of Homilies published in 1563, a quarter-century after the destruction of Gracechurch and its image, comparing Marian images to pagan goddesses:

> When you heare of our Lady of Walsyngham, our Lady of Ipswich, our Lady of Wylsdon, and such other: what is it but an imitation of the Gentyles idolaters? *Diana Agrotera, Diana Coriphea, Diana Ephesia, etc., Venus Cipria, Venus Paphia, Venus Gnidia.*[140]

After that, the active memory of Gracechurch, which till then still seemed threatening to Protestants, faded with the generation which had personally known it. Over the next decades, Ipswich became a model example of a Puritan-dominated urban corporation rather than a beacon for traditional pilgrimage. By 1573, the chapel building sounds to have been long demolished. In that year the Crown granted to two Stepney gentlemen a raft of so-called 'concealed lands', that is former church property whose existing owners had discovered (to their chagrin) was in their hands with shaky legal titles; this 'concealed lands' device was an easy way for the Crown to reward those to whom it owed favours, at other people's expense. Amid a vast array of small sums from former chantries and religious foundations, the new legal owners received a halfpenny rent from the land in Ipswich on which 'Our Lady of Graces chappell' had once been built. With a small historical irony, these two grantees, Edward Forthe and Henry Bett, were acting as agents for Thomas, second Lord Wentworth, son and heir of the man who had been the chief local agent in Gracechurch's destruction, and they were probably members of Wentworth's household.[141] Even though the Daundy almshouses in Lady Lane survived, it was a further symptom of changed times when in 1588 the Corporation made sale to the town Recorder (the leading Puritan lawyer John Clench) of the lands in Holbrook and Harkstead which had been bequeathed by Edmund Daundy partially for the purpose of supplying fuel to the inhabitants of his almshouses.[142]

St Matthew's church itself was briefly in danger in 1549, when in the age of rapid religious revolution under Edward VI, the borough of Ipswich evidently considered whether it should follow the example of York, Lincoln and Colchester and cull the numbers of its parish churches.[143] So on 22 November 1549, Katherine Meye, a widow of the parish of St Matthew, asked for burial in the parish church 'if it do continue a parish church wherein God may be praised': if not, she wished to be buried in the church of St Mary le Tower.[144] In the end, Ipswich, like the city of Exeter in the same period, seems to have abandoned thoughts of significant church closures, perhaps dreading another stimulus to unrest at a time when both corporations had been badly frightened by the popular commotions and rebellions of 1549.

Excerpt from Ogilby's map of Ipswich 1674.

As a result, St Matthew's and its splendid font are with us to the present day. Along with the reused sculptures and stones of the shrine at St Nicholas' church, they furnish our last original physical links to the shrine of Our Lady of Grace and its brief glory days in the early Tudor age. Yet Ipswich still

THREE-KINGS CT.
IPSWICH.

commemorates those lost marvels in more ways than it realises: not merely in the modern shrine in the Church of St Mary Elms, but in the name of the pub in Carr Street which still recalls the Angel Gabriel's Annunciation greeting to Our Lady full of Grace, the Salutation. Drinkers there might have been misled by its most recent pictorial inn-sign which showed two Victorian gentlemen greeting each other, but currently the pub gives no indication of what this name might mean. Perhaps one day, the Salutation may once more reveal just what an ancient story it preserves.

Three Kings Court by the Westgate [marked 3 on the map on p. 3]. Pen and ink and wash by Edward Charles Pococke (1846-1905) who had access to many 18th century drawings which are now long lost.

68

Appendix: Sir Robert Curson's narrative

Sir Robert, Lord Curson writes a full account of the events surrounding Mistress Wentworth of Gosfield and the shrine of Our Lady of Grace in Ipswich in 1516. It is here presented in modernised spelling, but otherwise preserves the words of the original; added material is in italics, except for reconstructed words. Original insertions in the text are indicated thus: <your>

BL Harleian MS 651, ff. 194v -196v

A miracle of our Blessed Lady of Grace at Ipswich

[*Page 1*] Pleaseth your noble grace to understand of a great miracle that was done the 15th day of April and the 7th year of <your> reign [*1516*] of King Henry VIII at Our Lady of Grace of Ipswich upon the daughter of Sir Roger Wentford [*Wentworth*] in Essex, a damsel of twelve years of age and as much from Hallowmas hither [*1 November 1515*] to on the Friday before Palm Sunday [*14 March 1516*] was in many ways vexed and troubled with the devil appearing to her so that she had utterly forgotten God [*original has 'good'*] and all his works, with marvellous great ragings, beating herself and doing all ills that she could unto them that were about her, making them greatly afraid and awaiting always if she might have got a knife to have killed herself. And after on our Lady Day in Easter Week by the might of God and of Our Lady, Our Lady appeared unto her in the picture and stature of the image of Our Lady of Grace in Ipswich. And in all her most [*i.e. worst*] rages when <she> had a sight of the image of our lady the first words she spake she said 'Oh Lady of Grace', and therewith the said devil went out of her sight and they that were about here asked of her 'Which Lady of Grace?' Her brother asked her if it were Our Lady of Grace of Cambridge and she shook her head. Another asked her if it were Our Lady of Grace of Ipswich [*page 2*] And she said 'yea, yea, let me be brought thither' and so she was brought thither the Sunday the 13th day of April [*recte 14 April*] and laid in the chapel at 3 of the clock [th]at afternoon before the image of Our Lady openly on a cheffon [*i.e. a litter or chair*] that every man might see in what case she was in. She might neither go ride, nor sit, she was so weak, and thus laying before Our Lady of Grace she was in the greatest torments that it was the most piteous sight that ever I saw. Her mouth was drawn unto her ear, her tongue out of her head her eyen [*i.e. eyes*] turned up that every [*i.e. each*] eye was as much as two eyen, her hands turned, [in *omitted*] her body every joint trembled, her colour often times as blue as azure. Thus she lay 3 hours the first night that she came thither and [at] six of the clock [*i.e. Angelus time*]

69

she came to her right shape and was a fair creature and then she said unto her keepers, 'This is the lady that appeared to me on Our Lady Day [*25 March 1516*]. Now I pray you have me to my lodging and bring me hither again tomorrow at six of the clock, for it is Our Lady's will that I shall be brought hither five times so that all people may see me young and old', and she was brought thither on the Monday [*14 April 1516*] by six of the clock and there was she laid before <Our Lady> and <as> soon as she was laid she stirred and was troubled as she was the first time unto noon, and then spake <she> 'Have me again before Our Lady till that it be four of the clock and then lay me again before Our Lady', and she was there raging and faring ill with herself as she did before and at six of the clock she was had again <to> her lodging. That was the third time and I am sure there was beyond a M [*1,000*] persons that saw the sight that same Sunday & Monday; and on the Tuesday [15 April 1516] she sent one of her keepers unto me by six of the clock beseeching me for God's sake that I would come to Our Lady of Grace bring[ing] with me as many as I could to pray for her to God and Our Lady. In like manner she sent unto the bailiffs of the town to be there and to bring with them as many as [they *omitted*] could, young <and> old, she said it was Our Lady's will that she should be holpen [*i.e. helped*] that day

before night. And so I and my wife went thither with as many as we could procure with the houses of religion [*i.e. the monasteries and friaries*] and other, and soo I was there from seven of the clock till it was eleven; and I am sure <there> was beyond a M [*thousand*] people the same day. And as for my part, I would not see any Christian creature in such trance and disfigurings of the body, head, mouth, ears, arms and hands so long as sessen [*?a season*] again for much good. About ten of the clock the Abbot of Bury came into the chapel and it was so full of people that I was fain to make many to void [*i.e. leave*] but if [*i.e. to make it possible that*] he might come in and so he came thither of pilgrimage on foot and he looked at the young gentlewoman. He said it was the most piteous sight that ever he saw and so he said there mass, and at eleven of the clock he went with me to dinner and there he made promise that if God and Our Lady would restore her to her right shape and fashion, he would seek Our Lady there every year on foot while he lived, and if he had thereto <hap> [*i.e. opportunity*]. As soon as he and I had dined he went to the Rood of Dovercourt and about [...] of the clock she sent to me again and desired me to come to Our Lady's chapel in Our Lady's name and in like case to the bailiffs and to cause as many as we could to come to [*erased?*] with us then she should surely be delivered from all her pains and torments, so [I sent to the religious] [*page 3*] houses and to the other and so there were a great people [*crowd*] assembled which went thither and found her there raging, her body and all her members disfigured as she was before and suddenly as we all were there man woman and child praying for her on our knees with many weeping tears, she came to herself suddenly in all her limbs and then was as fair a thing and right shapen as men may see. And then I asked her 'Mistress, how do you?' and she starte[d] up suddenly and kneeled down on [her] knees holding up her hands to her Lady and said 'My Lord Curson, I thank God, Our Lady and you, all good men and women of this country. By your good prayers now am I redeemed of all my pains and dolours by the help of Blessed Lady'. And on the next day she rode home behind a man to her father's whole and sound. So the said maiden made promise to Our Lady of Grace of Ipswich that she would come again unto her within eleven days after she came home to her father's [*i.e Saturday 26 April 1516?*]. So when the day was that she would set forwards on foot, she said 'Now I must depart father, and I pray [I pray *repeated*] you of your blessing that I may fulfill my promise unto our Blessed Lady of Grace' (though her father and her mother thought to have deferred the time unto Whitsuntide [*11 May 1516*] that at that time the most part of the worshipful of the country to come with her). So the due day [*original* 'day day'] was broken by them that she could not keep her promise she altered clean [*i.e. changed altogether*] and fell in a great sweat and sent for her father and mother, saying unto them both 'see here what you have done to me and put me again to these great pains because of breaking of my promise' and bade them 'choose whether ye would have me lie still in these pains' or else that they would promise her to go forth with her. And then her father and mother said 'Ye shall go, and we with you, on Thursday next with God's grace.' [*Thursday 1 May 1516; Ascension Day*] And with that word she called for her kirtle and bade nobody to help her rise, and so she rose in all the great sweat and sickness that all that were about her thought rather that she should have died then to [have *omitted*] lived. How be it, as soon as she was up she was whole and sound and said 'I shall not here give no answers to them that shall speak to me but I shall speak well enough myself and shall shew many marvels by the Holy Ghost and Our Blessed Lady of Grace of Ipswich, for whoso argues against it I can know them and will them to amend them shortly', and alway as she came apperceived any of those persons, she would say to them 'amend your living and ever be steadfast in the faith for at our lady of grace you shall know more'. So at the coming of her to Ipswich [*Friday 2 May 1516?*], the three houses of friars and the two houses of canons with all the parish priests of the town received her without the town with other gentlemen of the country, as myself, Sir Richard Wentworth, Sir William Waldegrave, Sir John Willoughby, Sir Thomas Tyrrell, Master Thomas Tay with many other gentlemen and their wives, I am sure beyond four thousand people with her father and mother. So she came and followed the cross, behaving herself [self *repeated*] full well and vertuously all the way unto the chapel of [*page 4*] of Our Lady of Grace and there she made her offering as discreetly as any creature could do and after that she had been there nigh an hour she departed home to her lodging which was nigh upon five of the clock. Many people prayed her for to take their offerings and pray for them unto God and to our blessed lady; of many she would not receive their offerings except they would be more steadfast in the faith than they were, for she said that there were many that believed not the miracles that our lady did on her, but trusted in god and our [Lady *omitted*] or [*ere*] she departed from her grace that they should have more cause to believe this, without [*mistake for* 'with'?] many other miraculous wordes she had to every man and woman after that she came to her lodging. And about twelve of the clock before midnight when the most part of the town were in rest

and suddenly she called certain persons unto her and gave to every [*each*] of them their charges and so one person of them she sent to me and to my wife, requiring us both in God's behalfe and Our Lady's that we would immediately come to her and I should see things that God and Our <Lady> would should be shewed that time and so she sent to Mr Wentworth and to Mr Waldegrave and to the Doctor [*Bailey*] and the best learned men and to the worshipful of the town and so by twelve of the clock at midnight I and all these persons were comen to her lodging and there she made a great and marvellous argument against the Doctor and other learned men and continued nigh a two hours and all in the faith so that no creature living except it had been by the Holy Ghost could have spoken such words as she did. So the Doctor said un[to *omitted*] her 'Ye have sent here for the honourable men here in presence, and said that they and all we should see great things, the which ye should shew by the might of the Holy Ghost and Our Lady.' She answered him 'An if ye and others would be steadfast in the faith. Sometime ye believe my words and sometime ye set little [store] by them', and therewith her mother said unto her 'Ah daughter, ye must take heed to the great clerks and of their saying' 'Yea Mother', quoth she, 'ye wot not what you speak. I say nothing but it is by the Holy Ghost's commandments and by Our Lady, and the which ye shall see what good ye alldo to me with your arguments, for I shall be by and by in the same case I was that day I was helpen by our Blessed Lady', and as she had said before us, she fell with her body her hands and her eyen and mouth all out of fashion [*shape*], which was piteous sight to see, so that all they that were there wept and made their prayers to God and Our Lady that she might come to her right shape again. So I took her a cross of gold of mine, which had on the one side Our Lady of Pity with her son in her lap and on the other side the blessed five wounds of Our Lord, and I put it into her hands, and as soon as she had it, she kissed it and blessed <them> therewith to the best of her power and thus continued nigh an hour. And suddenly one of her own sisters and another of her next kinswoman of her came out of their beds in their smocks as mad as any creatures could be with grievous noise, cryings and shriekings, and came straight unto her crying 'We believe, we believe, we doubt not, we doubt not', [*page 5*] and suddenly among them all she start[ed] up on feet in as good fashion and shape as ever she was and took her sister in her arms and kissed her and crossed her with the cross that was in her hand many times and bade her believe steadfastly in the faith, and by God's grace and our Lady's, she and her fellow should be safe

again and be forgiven of God and of Our Lady, so that they would be truly confessed, and incontinently these two persons came to their minds with great repentance; and as she was talking with us, her own brother John Wentford he fell down suddenly from himself with crying, raging and plucking [*i.e. tearing*] so that three or four men might scarcely hold him and so among all other she went to him and bade him remember the Passion of Christ and bade him believe steadfastly in the faith for that she did was by the might of ['the' *omitted*] Holy Ghost and Our Lady and he should be holpen and she crossed him, blessed him and kissed him and incontinently he came to himself and cried God mercy and Our Lady and her, that he had not believed better before, and immediately she desired all that were there, young and old, that they should be barefooted and bare legged to go to the chapel of our lady of <Grace> to give thanks to God and to Our Lady, and she said to me 'My lord, ere you come out of the chapel you shall see more miracles that our lady would should be done there.' So I with all the other that were there went with her about two of the clock in the morning, and so did her sister and brother which had been mad, and by that time that she and we had entered into the chapel, her brother was the most stark mad man that might be, despising God and Our Lady (and it was as much as four men

73

could hold him), calling to his father 'Where is that whoreson my father? If I might get him, I would kill him', and her sister fell again into a great tormenting and also three more fell out of their myndes, so that I and all other that were there weened [*believed*] the day of doom had become, so that well we [?*and*] them that might, get them ghostly fathers to be shriven, so this holy maiden, praying to God and to Our Lady, went to her sister and to the other gentlewoman. Through the might of God and Our Lady she redeemed them to their own good minds and again, and caused them to be shriven and then she came to her brother, crying unto him to believe truly on Jesus Christ and his mother Mary, and she would pray for him. He defied her, God and Our Lady and all their works, and would have plucked [*i.e. torn*] at her; and then this maid said unto them that held him, 'Let me alone with him', and so she took him in her arms and said unto him, 'Ye false man in the faith, let me see what you and the devil that is within you can do to me!' and blessed him with the holy candle [*i.e the Paschal candle*] and poured holy water in his mouth and he did spit it out; then she said 'I shall blow faith into you in spite of the devil', and so she opened his mouth and teeth, and did blow into his body, and shortly he began to come to himself and there this good maiden brought a ghostly [*i.e. spiritual*] father unto him to shrive him,

but is was long ere he would believe steadfastly; so she came again unto him asking him how he did. He said 'I thank God and Our Lady and you sister, I am safe', and therewith he fell asleep; and she covered him, desiring every man and woman to [go ?*lost*] home to their rests, and thanked god that her brother was safe, both body and soul; and so that same Sunday [*4 May 1516*] at two of the clock in the afternoon there was made a sermon by Doctor Bailey showing the miracles that were done by the power of [her *obscured?*] and by our Blessed Lady, and that they had given power to our blessed lady indeed, and that sith [*i.e. since*] England was christened, were never shewed such miracles. Laud, honour and praising be to God and to our blessed lady of grace, world without end Amen. Lack of parchment etc
Per [*By*] W H s[criptum *or* secretarium]

Abbreviations used in the notes

BL   British Library

CS   *Camden Society* publications

LP   *Letters and Papers, Foreign and Domestic, of the reign of Henry VIII, 1509-47*, ed. J.S. Brewer *et al.* (H.M.S.O., 21 vols. and 2 vols. addenda, 1862-1932)

NCC   Norfolk and Norwich Record Office, Norwich Consistory Court

ODNB   *Oxford Dictionary of National Biography*

PSIA   *Proceedings of the Suffolk Institute of Archaeology and History*

RSTC   *A Short Title Catalogue of Books printed in England, Scotland, and Ireland and of English Books Printed Abroad before the year 1640*, ed. A.W. Pollard and G.R. Redgrave, rev. W.A. Jackson and F.S. Ferguson and completed by K.F. Pantzer (The Bibliographical Society, 3 vols., 1976-91)

SROI   Suffolk Record Office, Ipswich

TNA (PRO)   The National Archives (Public Record Office), Kew

Notes

1. For details of the modern shrine and its devotional life, see http://www.stmaryattheelms.org.uk/st_mary_at_the_elms/Shrine.html, accessed 18 November 2012.

2. J. Foxe, *The first volume of the ecclesiasticall history contayning the actes [and] monumentes of thinges passed in euery kinges time, in this realme, especially in the Churche of England principally to be noted ...* (London, 1576, *RSTC* 11224), Book 8, p. 1074. This appears to be the first edition in which Foxe inserted a description of these events.

3. D. Dymond and E. Martin (eds), *An Historical Atlas of Suffolk* (Ipswich, 1988), 122-23; 2nd edition 1989, 158-59, gives conjectural placings for these various buildings, which we are now modifying. For All Saints and St George, see J. Kirby, *The Suffolk Traveller* (2d edn, London, 1764), pp. 43-44. The suggestion of the round tower for St George's church comes from the illustration of it at J. Foxe, *Actes and monuments of these latter and perillous dayes touching matters of the Church, wherein ar comprehended and decribed the great persecutions and horrible troubles, that haue bene wrought and practised by the Romishe prelates, speciallye in this realme of England and Scotlande, from the yeare of our Lorde a thousande, vnto the tyme nowe present ...* (London, 1563, RSTC 11222), p. 474, in the background of Thomas Bilney being pulled from the pulpit in 1527. This picture is by no means conclusive evidence, but it is worth future

archaeologists being alert to the possibility. Ogilby's map of 1674 shows the church without naming it (it was already redundant by then), and since Ogilby was meticulous in showing the actual footprints of buildings, it is significant that there is no evidence of a round tower in his depiction.

4. A. St. J. Story-Maskelyne *et al.* (eds), *Liber feodorum: The book of fees, commonly called Testa de Nevill, reformed from the earliest MSS (London, 1920)*, p. 283 [1219]: 'Ecclesia Sancti Mathei et ecclesia Omnium Sanctorum de Gypeswic' sunt de donatione domini regis et Johannes de Plessis est persona per dominum Regem Johannem ...'; p. 391 [1226-1228]: 'De ecclesiis dicunt quod ecclesia Sancti Martini [*sic*] et ecclesia Omnium sanctorum sunt de donacione domini regis et Henricus de Weston tenet eas de dono domini Regis.'

5. C. Morley, 'A check-list of the sacred buildings of Suffolk, to which are added gilds', *PSIA* XIX (1925-27), pp. 168-211, at p. 192, suggested that the shrine was mentioned in 1297, but this was a mistake, prompted by the mention of the marriage at F. Haslewood, 'Our Lady of Ipswich', *PSIA* X (1898-1900), pp. 53-55, at p. 53. Haslewood assumed that Gracechurch was the venue for the wedding in 1297 of Princess Elizabeth, daughter of King Edward I, to John, Count of Holland, which in fact took place in 'the King's Chapel' within the Priory of St Peter & St Paul, claimed by the Crown at that time. J. Wodderspoon, *Memorials of the Ancient Town of Ipswich* (Ipswich, 1850), pp. 245-254, provides a description of this visit, from the royal accounts in BL Additional MS 7965 (second foliation).

6. So in J. Bacon, *Liber Regis, vel Thesaurus Rerum Ecclesiasticarum* ... (London, 1786), p. 744, it is listed as 'All Saints Cur. In Ipswich, destructa.'

7. G. Martin (ed.), *The Ipswich Recognisance Rolls 1294-1327: a calendar* (Suffolk Record Society XVI, 1973), p. 60.

8. SROI, C/2/4/1/5. For an account of Halteby's murder in Ipswich in 1344, and for the demonstrations in the town against the royal justices indicting his murderers, see G.O. Sayles (ed.), *Select Cases in the Court of King's Bench under Edward III* (Selden Society LXXXII, 1965, no. 19, pp. 37-38.

9. SROI, C/2/4/1/27.

10. SROI, C/2/4/1/30. John and Philip Harneys had been prominent in Ipswich borough government in the late thirteenth century.

11. F. Haslewood, 'St Matthew's Church, Ipswich', *PSIA* VII (1887-89), pp. 129-208, at pp. 154-89, conveniently groups together the sequence of presentations to the rectory with much supporting documentation, though not always accurately transcribed or understood.

12. SROI, C/2/4/1/61.

13. *Calendar of entries in the Papal Registers relating to Great Britain and Ireland, 1198-* (20 vols so far, 1893-2005), II, p. 256 (*Regesta* 83, f. 142d). On Marian shrine indulgences, see D. Webb,

Pilgrimage in medieval England (London, 2000), 100. We are indebted to Martin Sanford for bringing these references to our attention.

14.   … 'ex speciali devotione Regis': W.M. Ormrod, 'The personal religion of Edward III', *Speculum* 64 (1989), 849-77, at p. 857, n. 46, citing TNA (PRO), E36/204, f. 72r.

15.   TNA (PRO), E101/404/11, m. 1, also cited in L.J. Redstone, *Ipswich through the ages* (Ipswich 1948), p. 111: 'In consimili oblacione domine ad missam celebratam in presencia sua ad quandam ymaginem pretiosam in capella extra muros ville de Yepeswich ultimo die Aprilis, iii s. iv d.' 'Pretiosam' is very faded, but this was Lilian Redstone's reading, and it seems right. Blanche's previous oblation had been in the Abbey of St John's Colchester on 26 April 1402, and her last recorded oblation in Ipswich was at Christ Church Priory on Corpus Christi day, 25 May 1402, before her next donation at mass in the Low Countries on 26 June. For a workmanlike account of Princess Blanche's journey towards her wedding, see J.H. Wylie, *History of England under Henry IV* (4 vols, London, 1884-98), I, pp. 252-56, which records her leaving Ipswich for Cologne on 21 June. We are indebted to Profs Nigel Saul and Chris Given-Wilson for their help in guiding us to these sources.

16.   Latimer to Cromwell, 13 June 1538: H. Ellis, *Original letters illustrative of English history …* 3rd series III (London, 1846), p. 207.

17.   Will of William Bele of Ipswich, made in 1479 and proved in 1487, SROI IC/AA1/3/48, and also quoted in Haslewood, 'St Matthew's Church, Ipswich', 198: 'corpus sepeliendum coram altare sanctae Katerinae in ecclesia sancti Mathei Apostoli Gipp'. Bele additionally left twelve pence to the high altar of St Matthew, and six shillings to the repair of the church, with a further bequest for masses at St Clement's Ipswich.

18.   SROI IC/AA2/2/15.

19.   NCC 239 Brosyard. The names are as unusual as that of Sayeena Leew, and one wonders whether the Velvets/Welwets were of Dutch or Low German extraction, also how they might relate to the Edmund Gelgate of a generation or two later, a lawyer who was among the early sixteenth-century bailiffs of the town. Alternatively we might be looking at a very local toponymic surname deriving from Gaolgate Lane beside the Bargate.

20.   J. Payne Collier (ed.), *Household books of John, Duke of Norfolk …* (Roxburghe Club, London, 1844), 62.

21.   For the Howard association with fifteenth-century Ipswich, see J.M. Blatchly, *A Famous Antient Seed-Plot of Learning: A History of Ipswich School* (Ipswich, 2003),15-20.

22.   Margery Paston to John Paston III: N. Davis (ed.), *Paston letters and papers of the fifteenth century* (3 vols., Oxford, 1971-2005), I, p. 664 (no. 417). The letter is dated 1 November, but the year is uncertain, within the range 1479-84.

23.   N.H. Nicholas (ed.), *The Privy Purse expenses of Elizabeth of York; Wardrobe Accounts of Edward the*

Fourth … (London, 1830), 3-4. The context makes it clear that this was a vicarious pilgrimage by Barton on behalf of the Queen; he was given travel expenses of tenpence a day for 27 days. For the reaction of Elizabeth and Henry VII to Arthur's death, see S.B. Chrimes, *Henry VII* (London, 1972), 302-4.

24. NCC 10 Sayve, but also recorded in TNA (PRO), PCC 13 Morton II; and inaccurately pr. in Haslewood, 'Our Lady of Ipswich', pp. 54-55. Mynot does not seem to have held major office in Ipswich.

25. N. Bacon, ed. W.H. Richardson, *Annalls of Ipswiche* (Ipswich, 1884), 171, based on SROI, Ipswich Borough Archives, C/3/8/8/16. Perhaps this path could be identified with the path from near the shrine site to the parish church of St Matthew and later known as the 'Church Waye'.

26. Richard Bailey's will is TNA (PRO), PROB 11/14, f. 321v. For Robert Bailey as Fellow, see the listings of Fellows from 1510 and 1511, BL Additional MS 40070, ff. 46r, 73r, and for the Weybread relationship, below, n. 29.

27. For biographical details of Bailey, A.B. Emden, *A biographical register of the University of Cambridge to 1500* (Cambridge, 1963), p. 45, s.v. Bayly, John; Haslewood, 'St Matthew's Church, Ipswich', pp. 160-2. Wolsey's birth-year is indicated by the story recorded by George Cavendish that on 'Maundy Thursday [1530] he made his Maundy there [at Peterborough Abbey], in Our Lady's chapel, having fifty-nine poor men, whose feet he then washed, wiped and kissed': R. Lockyer (ed.),

Thomas Wolsey: his life and death written by George Cavendish his gentleman-usher (London, 1973), 172. Wolsey was therefore fifty-nine years of age in 1530.

28. The presentation is at *LP* I, no. 563/20. The unnamed previous incumbent was not John Master, who was to die sometime after 1520 and to whom there were bequests between 1506 and 1520 as curate in the parish; it was probably Edward Assheton (see n. 35 below). The institution is recorded in Norfolk and Norwich Record Office, Reg/9/15, f. 66v: Bailey was recorded as a D.D., and his sureties for the payment of first-fruits were named as William Hert, citizen and alderman of Norwich, and John Wylde of Ipswich, fletcher.

29. For the Weybread relationship to the Baileys, see Dr Bailey's regrant as a trustee of Mettingham College lands, dated from Mettingham, 1 August 1517, BL Additional Charters 63602. These lands became involved in a long-running lawsuit between the College and the Weybreads: see TNA (PRO), C1/729/36. For a gift from the Master of Mettingham to a servant of Dr Bailey in 1509, BL, Additional MS 40070, f. 33r, and for his association with Fellows of Mettingham in a sale at Covehithe, TNA (PRO), C1/736/59.

30. See payments to Bailey for the sermons and celebrating masses for Braunche in the accounts of Braunche's executors, BL, Additional MS 40061, f. 73r. Braunche's will is BL Additional Charters 37443.

31. *LP* III, no. 2483, p. 1048.

32. John Bailey's will is TNA (PRO), PROB 11/21 ff. 287-88. On the stone, see the notes of D.E. Davy, BL, Additional MS 19094, f. 84r.

33. *Calendar of Papal Registers* XIII pt i, pp. 6-7 and pt ii, pp. 696-97. Emden, *A biographical register of the University of Cambridge to 1500*, pp. 79-80, s.v. Bothe, Robert, details his career and exceptional pluralism.

34. Haslewood, 'St Matthew's Church, Ipswich', 159.

35. *Calendar of Papal Registers* XVI, no. 246, though perhaps following the original mistake of an Italian papal lawyer who had difficulty with the English name 'Assheton', they have read the surname as 'Allheron' or 'Assheron'. Assheton entered in Canon Law in 1476-77 and was admitted as Bachelor of Canon Law in 1479. Emden has split his identity between two people: Emden, *A biographical register of the University of Cambridge to 1500*, pp. 18, 20, s.v. Asheton, Edmund and Assheton, Edward. He is not to be confused with a younger Edmund Ashton who continued his career in Cambridge with theological studies rather than canon law, and was one of Thomas Cranmer's colleagues at Jesus College: see his nuncupative will of probably 1529, Cambridge University Library, University Archive Wills, I f. 49r, and J. and S.A. Venn (eds.), *Alumni Cantabrigienses* (4 vols., Cambridge, 1922-7), I, p. 46, s.v. Ashton, Edmund.

36. For court barons presided over by Assheton between 1515 and 1520, see Greater Manchester County Record Office, E7/1/1-3; there are several other witnesses to Assheton's participation in family affairs in Lancashire in these papers.

37. E. Duffy, *The Stripping of the Altars: traditional religion in England 1400-1580* (New Haven and London, 1992), 249-56.

38. TNA (PRO), PROB 11/8, ff. 155-57 (PCC 20 Holder), and see the record and fate of Daundy's bequest of land in SROI, C/3/10/2/1, 1 and 2 and SROI C/4/1/4 ff. 173-175, listed D. Allen (ed.), *Ipswich Borough Archives 1255-1835: a catalogue* (SRS 43, 2000), pp. 333-34, 419. There are leases of these lands in 1550: SROI, C/3/10/5/1 1 and 2, Allen (ed.), *Ipswich Borough Archives 1255-1835: a catalogue*, pp. 399-400.

39. BL MS Harley 651, ff. 194v-196v, a contemporary clerk's copy initialled 'W.H.s[*criptum*, or possibly but with less likelihood, *secretarium*]' but narrated in the first person by Curson. For the full text in modernised English, see below. As noted below, this MS copy is likely to have been made from a printed version of Curson's original. One of the present authors has provided a biography of Curson: J.M. Blatchly, *ODNB* s.v. 'Curson, Robert'; see also John Blatchly and Bill Haward, 'Sir Robert, Lord Curson, soldier, courtier and spy, and his Ipswich mansion', *PSIA* XLI (2007), 335-50.

40. The treatise, f. 194v, is addressed to 'your nobyle grace', and goes on to speak of 'yo'r Reynge of Kyng Hary the VIIIth'. The latter is an odd and unnatural phrase, especially as 'yo'r' appears to be interpolated in the same hand, and that might suggest that the original had 'ye', i.e. 'the', which

would make the recipient someone other than the King: either Cardinal Wolsey or one of England's two Dukes, Norfolk and Suffolk, all of whom were habitually styled 'Your Grace'. Without 'yo'r', the latter interpretation would be most likely, but perhaps 'of Kyng Hary the VIIIth' had been clumsily added by the printer.

41. [W. de Worde], *The myracles of our lady* (London, 1514, *RSTC* 17540), sig. C8r. The earlier edition is [W. de Worde], *The myracles of oure blessyd lady* (London, 1496, *RSTC* 17539), and the 1530 edition is *RSTC* 17541.

42. F. Madan, 'The daily ledger of John Dorne, 1529', in C.R.L. Fletcher (ed.), *Collectanea* Oxford Historical Society Publications 1st ser. V (1885), p,. 86, l. 257. At the same time, Dorne was also selling 'the mirackes of oree lady', for 4d (p. 119, l. 1193): this more expensive and substantial work must have been de Worde's *The myracles of our lady* in its 1514 edition.

43. BL Harley MS 651 has an inscription 'De monasterio s'c'e marie de Radyngie' at f. 3r. The account of the Ipswich miracle is the last item in the volume and is on a different and smaller gathering of pages, which begins at f. 192 with a short fifteenth-century world chronicle; the miracle story is copied straight after this in a different and slightly later hand, half way down f. 194v.

44. D.E. Davy recorded seeing the inscription for Smith on the back of a choir-stall in the chancel of St Matthew's in 1824: BL Additional MS 19094, f. 82v: 'John: Smyth : Pewterer : which : decessed :

the : xviij day : of : May : ye yere of : o'r Lord God, mccccxvj'. The unusual nature of the inscription is underlined by the fact that it does not incorporate a soul prayer. Smith's will is NCC 112-114 Spurling; it was made on 16 May 1516 and proved only a week later (23 May). Smith asked for burial in St Matthew's before the altar of St Erasmus and left money for a vestment set for the church, but makes no mention of the choir-stalls. Some fragments of what must be the same stallwork, rediscovered in the church tool-house not long before, are illustrated and described by Haslewood, 'St Matthew's Church, Ipswich', pp. 144-46.

45. NCC 23 Briggs: Brigges was clearly an enthusiast for pilgrimage, leaving his nephew and will-witness Thomas Brigges 3s 4d to go on a comparatively modest pilgrimage to St Etheldreda's shrine at Ely. It is tempting to see the 'many women' who are mentioned beside the four male witnesses as inmates of Daundy's almshouses. For Master, see references to him between 1506 and 1520, Haslewood, 'St Matthew's Church, Ipswich', pp. 159, 200, 201. There is no overlap in personnel between the wills of Smith and Brigges.

46. T. More, *A dyaloge of syr Thomas More knyghte ... Wherin be treated dyuers maters, as of the veneration and worshyp of ymages and relyques, prayng to sayntys, and goyng on pylgrymage. Wyth many othere thyngys touching the pestylent sect of Luther and Tyndale* (London, 1529, *RSTC* 18084), f. 20rv. A good modern edition is T. More, ed. T.M.C.

Lawler *et al.*, *A Dialogue concerning Heresies* (Yale, 1981: *Complete works of St Thomas More* VI pt i), pp. 92-96. Tyndale twice referred to the Gracechurch miracle, first in his *Obedience of a Christian Man* in 1527, provoking More into this reply of 1529, and then in 1530 in riposte to More's defence; neither of Tyndale's texts provides any independent information. See *Doctrinal Treatises and introductions to different portions of the Holy Scriptures. By William Tyndale ...*, ed. H. Walter (Parker Society, 1848), p. 327, and *An Answer to Sir Thomas More's Dialogue, the Supper of the Lord...and William Tracy's Testament expounded. By William Tyndale ...*, ed. H. Walter (P.S., 1850), pp. 89-92.

47. BL Additional MS 24435, f. 80rv.

48. *LP* II pt ii, Appendix no. 38, in which Wolsey tells the King that he will set out on the following Monday: dateable to the first week in September 1517 (*pace* the August dating by the editors of *LP*) by reference to Giustiani's despatch to Venice on 31 August 1517, *LP* II pt ii, no. 3655. Wolsey therefore began or intended to begin his journey on Monday 7 September.

49. *LP* IV pt iii, no. 5750, p. 2560.

50. D. MacCulloch, *Suffolk and the Tudors: politics and religion in an English county 1500-1600* (Oxford, 1986), pp. 137, 145, 151.

51. Wodderspoon, *Memorials of the Ancient Town of Ipswich*, p. 256; Wodderspoon does not reference his source. There is nothing in Bacon, ed. Richardson, *Annalls of Ipswiche*, on this visit, and that reflects the apparent lack of reference to it in surviving borough archives. To judge by royal grants, the King was at Newhall in Essex on 7 October 1522 (*LP* III pt ii no. 2601), and back there again on 14 October (*LP* III pt ii no. 2648/14). On the Norfolk stage of his visit, see N. Samman, 'The progresses of Henry VIII, 1509-1529', in D. MacCulloch (ed), *Henry VIII: politics, policy and piety* (Basingstoke, 1995), 59-74, at pp. 71, 261, citing the King's entertainment at Raynham Hall by Sir Roger Townsend, BL Additional MS 27449, f. 10.

52. SROI, C1/1/20.

53. TNA (PRO), SP 1/242/3 (*LP* Appendix I pt ii, no. 1312).

54. For gifts from Curson to the King in 1532 (twelve swans) and from the King in 1533 (a gilt cup), see respectively *LP* V, no. 686, p. 328 and *LP* VI, no. 32, p. 14. Such lists do not survive from every year of the reign, and there may well have been other exchanges.

55. Licence for the Assumption's inn-sign was granted at the Court held on the Friday before Ascension Day 20 Henry VIII (15 May 1528): SROI C/2/10/3/9, p. 216. A useful discussion is C.H. Evelyn White, 'The old inns and taverns of Ipswich: their memories and associations' *PSIA* VI (1886), 136-183, at 161 and 165.

56. The best account of the networks of publicity around Barton is E. Shagan, 'Print, orality and communications in the Maid of Kent Affair', *Journal of Ecclesiastical History* 52 (2001), 21-33.

57. J. Bale, *A mysterye of inyquyte contayned within the heretycall genealogye of Ponce Pantolabus ...* ([Antwerp], 1545, *RSTC* 1303): f. 30r.

58. R. Rex, *ODNB*, s.v. Wentworth, Jane; her will, as of Framlingham, gentlewoman, is SROI, IC/AA1/22/18.

59. TNA (PRO), SP1/54/7-9 (*LP* IV pt ii, no. 5556-7): Margery Calthorp was in dispute with her Nettlestead 'cousin' Sir Richard Wentworth over a pension he owed her.

60. *The Visitation of Suffolk 1561*, ed. J. Corder (Harleian Society, new ser. II-III, 1981, 1984), I, pp. 162-68.

61. In her will, Jane mentions a godson John Rous and a god-daughter Jane, but it has not been possible to fit these two into the Rous family tree: the Rous family was closely allied to Sir Nicholas Hare of Bruisyard, who had bought the nunnery and left a legacy to Jane Wentworth among other ex-nuns in his will of 1557, TNA (PRO) PROB 11/39, f. 46 (PCC 46 Wrastley).

62. W.L. Rutton, *Three branches of the family of Wentworth* (London, 1891), pp. 150, 153, 193; the family was originally a cadet branch of the well-known Yorkshire gentry and later noble family.

63. [Anon.], *A confutation of vnwritten verities both bi the holye scriptures and moste auncient autors ... translated and set forth, by E.P.* (Wesel, 1556, *RSTC* 5996), sig. 02r, amplifying material in Cranmer's theological notebooks, Royal 7B XII, which mention 'Agnes' Barton and Anne Wentworth at f.149. One of the co-authors, D. MacCulloch, *Thomas Cranmer: a life* (New Haven and London, 1996), 633-36, argues that the compiler/editor of the *Confutation* is Dr Stephen Nevinson, one of Cranmer's estate officials, Westmorland-born but educated in Cambridge and later resident in Kent.

64. F.G. Emmison (ed.), *Essex Wills: the Commissary Court 1558-1567* (Chelmsford, 1993), 155 (no. 734).

65. TNA (PRO), PROB 11/428/253 (PCC 24 Chaynay).

66. M. Bateson (ed.), 'A collection of original letters to the Privy Council, 1564 ...', *Camden Miscellany* 9 (Camden New Series, LIII, 1893), 1-75, at 62.

67. TNA (PRO), PROB 11/49, ff. 211-13. On Waldegrave and Cordell, see MacCulloch, *Suffolk and the Tudors*, 40, 88-89, 183-84, 240, 263, 267, 273. On Rooke Greene, see W.R. Trimble, *The Catholic laity in Elizabethan England 1558-1603* (Cambridge MA, 1964), 94-95, 144, 154, 202, 245, 249.

68. P. Morant, *The History and Antiquities of the County of Essex* (2 vols., 1763, 1768 [repr. Wakefield: EP Publishing, 1978]), ii, pp. 286, 525.

69. TNA (PRO), SP1/235, ff. 133-34 (*LP* Appendix, I pt i, no. 522): the only evidence of dating is the reference to 'My Lord Cardinal' in Bugges's recorded riposte, though an annotated National Archives copy of *LP* suggests 1526. Shaa died on 24 March 1532, leaving a four-year-old daughter Alice: Morant, *History and Antiquities of the County of Essex*, I, p. 217. It may not be without relevance that Shaa made an unusually long lease of Mark-Hall in Nettlewell, 99 years, to Henry Parker,

Lord Morley: ibid. II, p. 488. There are references to the Bugges, including to Edward, as a gentry family of Harlow, very near Nettlewell: ibid. II, pp. 483-85.

70. For Dowsing's visit to St Matthew's Ipswich, and comment on it, see T. Cooper (ed.), *The Journal of William Dowsing: iconoclasm in East Anglia during the English Civil War* (Woodbridge, 2001), p. 230 (no. 80).

71. Wodderspoon, *Memorials of the Ancient Town of Ipswich*, p. 386. Davy's account of the font is BL MS Additional 19094, f. 82v.

72. J. Newman, 'Cardinal Wolsey's collegiate foundations', in S.J. Gunn and P.G. Lindley (eds.), *Cardinal Wolsey: Church, State and Art* (Cambridge, 1991), 103-15, at p. 108.

73. BL MS Cotton Vitellius B.IV, f. 181 (*LP* III pt ii no. 1642).

74. Haslewood, 'St Matthew's Church, Ipswich', p. 161.

75. TNA (PRO), PROB 11/14, f. 321v.

76. On Cardinal College Oxford's letters patent of foundation, see *LP* IV pt i, nos 2151, 2152; for the letter of Ghinucci and Casale, *LP* IV pt i, no. 2158.

77. Cromwell to Thomas Arundel, 30 June 1528: *LP* IV pt ii, no. 4697.

78. On Winter's grant of arms, Haslewood, 'St Matthew's Church, Ipswich', p. 163; we are grateful to Christopher Fletcher-Vane, Portcullis Pursuivant, for providing us with details of the heraldry for Winter (College of Arms MSS, W.Z.

274 and EDN 56/66). Joan Larke, Wolsey's mistress and Winter's mother, was sister to a previous Archdeacon of Sudbury (1517-22), Thomas Larke, royal civil servant and also sometime Master of Trinity Hall, Cambridge; she also gained a grant of arms, College of Arms MSS: Miscellaneous Grants II/113. On appointments as Archdeacon of Suffolk, J. Le Neve, *Fasti Ecclesiae Anglicanae 1300-1541: Monastic Cathedrals* (London, 1963), p. 34, and MacCulloch, *Suffolk and the Tudors*, p. 131.

79. TNA (PRO), E135/17/11.

80. MacCulloch, *Suffolk and the Tudors,* 151.

81. *LP* IV pt ii no. 4423, with a follow-up stage in the grant on 29 July 1528, *LP* IV pt ii, no. 4574.

82. *LP* IV pt ii no. 4435, 29 June 1528.

83. In a letter dateable to March 1528, the Duke of Norfolk wrote to Wolsey reporting that he had commissioned a plan of St Peter's Priory, and hoped that his advice would save the Cardinal money there, which sounds as if Wolsey had already decided to fix on St Peter's at least for his initial foundation: TNA (PRO) SP 1/47 f. 83v (*LP* IV pt ii no. 4044).

84. BL Cotton MS Vespasian F XIII, f. 250 (*LP* IV iii, no. 5505).

85. BL MS Cotton Titus B.1, f. 281 (*LP* IV pt. ii, no. 4778); printed *in extenso* in *Original Letters illustrative of English History ... from autographs in the British Museum and ... other collections*, ed. H. Ellis (11 vols. in 3 series: London, 1824, 1827, 1846), series I vol. 1, pp. 185f.

86. 'Mr Wentford' might be thought to be Sir Roger Wentworth, father of the Maid of Ipswich, but Capon specifically referred in his listing to the gentlemen of the shire (i.e. Suffolk), which means that 'Mr Wentford' can only refer to Sir Thomas Wentworth. Sir Thomas was granted a barony in 1529. Curson's absence from this ceremony is as mysterious as the absence of any gift to the shrine in his will of 1535, when the old man was punctilious in leaving generous donations to all the Ipswich friaries: NCC 287 Attmere.

87. Illustrated in Gunn and Lindley, *Wolsey*, no. 6, from TNA (PRO), E24/23/15, and from another copy in Blatchly, *A Famous Antient Seed-Plot of Learning: A History of Ipswich School*, 30.

88. *LP* V, no. 1351.

89. SROI, C/3/8/7/10, listed Allen (ed.), *Ipswich Borough Archives 1255-1835: a catalogue*, p. 306.

90. TNA (PRO), PROB 11/26, ff. 33-34 (PCC 5 Crumwell). The font at St Peter's is a bulky square Romanesque specimen with Tournai marble bowl; any cover for it would have needed radical adjustment for the octagonal font of St Matthew's.

91. BL MS Additional 19094, f. 82v.

92. Foxe, *Actes and monuments of these latter and perillous dayes ...* (1563, *RSTC* 11222), pp. 473-74 [the pagination has skipped two leaves before this]. It is interesting that Bilney's contemptuous list of chief shrines is the same as the first three items on the wish-list of four shrines to which a poor singlewoman of Ipswich St Peter's had requested pilgrimage in the previous year: Ipswich, Walsingham and Canterbury, with a fourth option to 'St Cornelys' in London, perhaps a garbled form of the chapel of St Thomas Acon (the Mercers' Chapel, dedicated to Thomas Becket). Joan Keyn's will, made 27 July 1526, was never proved for lack of goods: NNRO, NCC 186 Groundesborough.

93. *LP* IV, pt ii, no. 4029(2), citing BL Harley 421, f. 17: confession of John Pykas.

94. *LP* IV, pt ii, no. 4175(3), citing BL Harley 421, f. 24: confession of William Raylond of Colchester.

95. *LP* IV, pt ii, no. 4545, citing BL Harley 421, f. 28: confession of Edmund Tyball of Steeple Bumpstead.

96. *LP* IV, pt ii, no. 4242, citation from J. Strype, *Ecclesiastical Memorials ...* (3 vols, London, 1721), I pt ii, no. 18 (pp. 39-40).

97. *LP* IV, pt ii, no. 4529(3), citing BL Harley 421, f. 15. For a further sneer from John Tyball's confession, see *LP* IV, pt ii, no. 4218.

98. *LP* IV, pt ii, no. 4850, citing BL Harley 421, f. 34. Since St Peter's Priory was no longer a monastery by the time of this judgement, the only candidate in Ipswich for being mistaken for an 'abbey' was Holy Trinity/Christ Church: perhaps chosen because Bilney had preached one of the most prominent sermons of his campaign there.

99. More, *A dyaloge*, f. 22r.

100. *An Answer to Sir Thomas More's Dialogue, the Supper of the Lord...and William Tracy's Testament*

expounded. By William Tyndale ..., ed. H. Walter (P.S., 1850), pp. 89-92.

101. MacCulloch, *Suffolk and the Tudors*, p. 155. Most of the vandalism, including an extended account of the destruction of the Rood of Dovercourt by men from Dedham, is recorded in Foxe, *Actes and monuments of these latter and perillous dayes* ... (1563, *RSTC* 11222), pp. 495-96. The reference to the Ipswich cross is only recorded by the Butley Priory Chronicler, under 1531: A.G. Dickens, *Late Monasticism and the Reformation* (London and Rio Grande, 1994), p. 60. It may nevertheless be also disguised in Foxe, p. 496, under the confusion of a reference to the destruction of a second image of St Petronilla 'in a chapel by Ipswich' besides a first St Petronilla at Great Horkesley: the Butley Chronicle only refers to a crucifix 'apud Sanctam Petronillam', after its reference to a crucifix at St Mary of Ipswich.

102. C.H. Evelyn White, 'The "Stoneing Cross" of Dowsing's Journal, an inquiry into the meaning and application of the term, with some remarks on the ancient stone crosses of Ipswich', *PSIA* VI (1885), 1-8, at pp. 3-5.

103. TNA (PRO), SP 1/84/159 (*LP* VII, no. 803); 6 June [1534]. In 1529 Rush had been the bearer of an important letter to Wolsey from Curson, in which Curson, desperately trying to stop Wolsey compulsorily purchasing his Ipswich mansion, described him as his 'felowe' [intimate]: BL Cotton MS Vespasian F XIII, f. 250 (*LP* IV iii, no. 5505).

104. On Crewkhorne and Pembroke Hall, see C.H. and T. Cooper (eds), *Athenae Cantabrigienses I: 1500-1525* (Cambridge, 1858), 72. His dispensations in the 1530s to retain a cap when preaching and being made DD suggests that his health was frail at that stage, though he contrived to live until 1558. For his service with the Dowager Countess of Oxford, see J. Ward, 'Elizabeth Beaumont, Countess of Oxford (d. 1537): her life and connections', *Transactions of the Monumental Brass Society* XVII (2003-5), 1-13, at p. 9, and for her nun relatives, ibid., pp. 5 and 13. On Katherine Christmas and her mother Muriel Christmas, ibid., pp. 8-9, and for an encomium to Muriel from another exuberantly Catholic source, D. MacCulloch (ed.) 'The *Vita Mariae Angliae Reginae* of Robert Wingfield of Brantham', (*Camden Miscellany* 28, CS 4th ser. 29, 1984), pp. 181-301, at pp. 221, 270, 298.

105. BL Cotton MS Cleopatra E IV, f. 110, pr. in T. Wright (ed), *Three Chapters of Letters relating to the Suppression of Monasteries* (CS 1st ser. 26, 1843), p. 36; *LP* X, no. 462.

106. [M. Bucer], *A treatise declaryng and shewig [sic] dyuers causes taken out of the holy scriptures of the sentences of holy faders and of the decrees of deuout emperours, that pyctures and other ymages which were wont to be worshypped, ar in no wise to be suffred in the temples or churches of Christen men* ... (London, ?1535, *RSTC* 24239), sig. D4v. See M. Aston, *England's Iconoclasts. I. Laws against Images* (Oxford: Clarendon Press, 1988), pp. 203-10.

107. [Bucer], *A treatise*, sig. B3v.

108. BL Cotton MS Cleopatra E IV, f. 229, pr. *Three Chapters of Letters relating to the Suppression of Monasteries*, ed. Wright, p. 144; *LP* XIII pt i, no. 192).

109. P. Marshall, 'The rood of Boxley, the Blood of Hailes and the defence of the Henrician Church', *Journal of Ecclesiastical History* 46 (1995), pp. 689-96. Aston, *England's Iconoclasts*, p. 234, confuses the date of the destruction of the images of Walsingham and Ipswich with their arrival in London in July.

110. TNA (PRO), SP 1/242/3 (*LP* Appendix I pt ii, no. 1312).

111. SROI, IC/AA1/10/83. There is a puzzle in that the payments regarding furnishings and plate of Gracechurch recorded in Cromwell's accounts as being made by William Lawrence, without any qualification about his decease, are dated in the following year, 1539: *LP* XIV pt ii, no. 782, pp. 325, 328. This same Lawrence also paid a twenty-mark annual fee for the late College in Ipswich, that is Wolsey's College, in 1536, 1537, 1538 and 1539: ibid, pp. 319, 321, 324, 328. There can be no mistake in the date of probate of the will, which for mysterious reasons was carried out twice, once on 14 August 1538 and again on 1 October 1538.

112. Latimer to Cromwell, 13 June 1538: Ellis, *Original Letters...* 3rd series III, p. 207 (*LP* XIII pt i, no. 1177).

113. Lawrence to Cromwell, undated: TNA (PRO), SP 1/242/5; Ellis, *Original Letters...* 3rd series III, p. 78 (*LP* Appendix I pt ii, no. 1313).

114. Thacker to Cromwell, 30 July 1538: Ellis, *Original Letters...* 3rd series III, p. 79 (*LP* XIII pt i, no. 1501). Accordingly, the image of Our Lady at Nettuno in Italy has been furnished with silver shoes.

115. Thacker to Cromwell, 1 September 1538: Ellis, *Original Letters...* 3rd series III, p. 100 (*LP* XIII ii, no. 256).

116. *A Chronicle of England ... by Charles Wriothesley, Windsor Herald*, ed. W.D. Hamilton (2 vols., Camden Society, 2nd ser. 11, 20, 1875, 1877), I, p. 83. It is easy to mistake Wriothesley's wording as Margaret Aston did (above, n. 109), and assume that the images were burned when they arrived in July; but the chronology just outlined shows that this is impossible.

117. MacCulloch, *Suffolk and the Tudors*, 160.

118. J. Bale, *A comedy concernynge thre lawes, of nature Moses, & Christ, corrupted by the sodomytes. Pharysees and Papystes* (Wesel, ?1547, RSTC 1287), sig. C4r. The colophon at sig. G4r says explicitly that the play was 'compyled by Johan Bale. Anno MDXXXVIII, and lately inprented per Nicolaum Bamburgensem', implying a caesura between composition and publication. This particular scene assumes *inter alia* that the London Minoresses is as yet undissolved, which would have been the case in 1538, and the whole ambience of the play is of a half-reformed church appropriate to that era. A reference to 'Yngham

Trynyte' at sig. D2r is a remarkable East Anglian in-joke about the Trinitarian Norfolk priory of Ingham irregularly dissolved in 1536, which could not have had currency much later than 1538. The date of publication after 1538 is not at all certain, but it is likely to have been 1547, like Bale's other surviving plays. In the patently topically-adjusted material at the end, the reader is exhorted at sig. G1r to 'praye for quene Kateryne [Parr], and the noble lord protectour,' which puts it in the timeframe 1547-48.

119. A further passing reference in verse to Our Lady of Ipswich comes in the course of a formidably long gazetteer of destroyed shrines in a propaganda poem by one of Cromwell's servants, William Gray of Reading, 'A booke intituled the fantasie of Idolatrie', evidently written in 1538 or early 1539, and first preserved in Foxe, *Actes and monuments of these latter and perillous dayes ...* (1563, *RSTC* 11222), pp. 599-600.

120. Cromwell's receipts, *LP* XIV pt ii, no. 782, pp. 325, 328.

121. Allen (ed.), *Ipswich Borough Archives 1255-1835: a catalogue*, p. 522.

122. Sabyn and Nottingham to Cromwell, 20 March s.a., TNA (PRO), SP 1/117/65-66 (*LP* XII pt i, no. 688. This letter is there dated to 1537, but that cannot be right: Sabyn and Nottingham are described in it as bailiffs, in which office, according to Bacon, ed. Richardson, *Annalls of Ipswiche*, p. 214, they served in the year beginning 8 September 1539; so a letter from them as bailiffs dated 20 March can only be of 1540. Cromwell was not yet Earl of Essex, being created Earl on 17 April 1540, and would be executed on 28 July 1540. On Argentine's chequered and eventful career, see J.M. Blatchly, *ODNB* s.v. 'Argentine [*formerly* Sexton], Richard'.

123. Lawrence to Cromwell, 1538, TNA (PRO), SP 1/242/3 (*LP* Appendix, I pt.ii, no. 1312); petition of parishioners of St Peter's, TNA (PRO), SP 1/240/227 (*LP* Appendix, I pt. i, no. 1171), undated, but probably of 1538.

124. The case is presented but not endorsed in S. Smith, *The Madonna of Ipswich* (Ipswich, 1980). Sensible remarks *per contra*, with which we concur, are to be found in G. Waller, *The Virgin Mary in late medieval and early modern English literature and popular culture* (New York, 2011), 1-2.

125. There is extensive treatment of the sculptures in K.J. Galbraith, 'Early sculptures at St Nicholas' Church, Ipswich', *PSIA* 31 (1970), pp. 172-84; Galbraith, 'Further thoughts on the boar at St Nicholas; Church, Ipswich', *PSIA* 33 (1976), pp. 68-74; E. Okasha, 'Some lost Anglo-Saxon inscriptions from St Nicholas; Church, Ipswich', 80-84. Building on all this, S.J. Plunkett, 'Appendix: Anglo-Saxon Stone Sculpture and Architecture in Suffolk', in S. West, *A Corpus of Anglo-Saxon Material from Suffolk* (Ipswich, 1998), pp. 328-357, esp. 328-29, 338-341, 356, offers the best present overview.

126. BL Additional MS, 19094 fo 121r: 'In the wall, on the outside, at the west end of the south aisle, are two pieces of ancient sculpture, on stone; one

represents an angel in a loose dress with a sword & shield & wings attacking a dragon, below this is an inscription but it is too high to be made out without assistance, - this is in a square - the other represents a boar feeding, he is semi circular'. See also Kirby, *The Suffolk Traveller*, (2nd edition. London 1764), pp. 45-46: a notice of the St Michael panel.

127. On the dating of the church, see B. Haward, *Suffolk Medieval Church Arcades* ... (Ipswich, 1993), pp. 30, 130, 280-81.

128. BL, MS Additional 41305, f. 155rv (we are grateful to David Dymond for drawing our attention to this). The rental forms a discrete section, ff. 145-56, of a composite volume labeled (at f. 1r) 'Her is the Boke off certeyn Bargeynes Tempore d'ne Alianore Touneshend vidue'. Lady Eleanor may be identifiable as Eleanor daughter of Sir John Heydon who married John Townshend of Raynham in 1511/12. He died in 1540: see C. Moreton, *The Townshends and their world: gentry, law, and land in Norfolk c. 1450-1551* 38-39. She seems still to have been alive in 1572, to judge from an acquittance to her and her grandson Sir Roger Townshend, Folger Shakespeare Library, Washington DC, MS L.d.793, but this rental is shown to date before 1550 by its mention at ff. 149r and 150v of lands in the hands of Sir Robert Lytton of Shrubland Hall, who died in that year.

129. NCC 287 Attmere.

130. TNA (PRO), E36/153, p. 219 (*LP* XIII pt i, no. 699, p. 266).

131. The story was first excavated by John Webb, 'Sir Robert Curson of Ipswich: a minor mystery solved', *Suffolk Institute of Archaeology and History Newsletter* 32 (Spring 1991), 9-10. The Churchwardens' accounts are BL Additional MS 25344; we are very grateful to Roger and Stella Wolfe for making available to us their transcript of these accounts. Dame Margaret's gift to the church in 1566 is BL Additional MS 25344, f. 10r, and her executors in 1579 paid £2.6s 8d 'for hir grave place', compared with the customary 6s 8d (ibid., f. 19r). Her will is TNA (PRO), PROB 11/59/550, calendared in F G Emmison, *Elizabethan Life IV, Gentry Wills of Essex Gentry and Merchants* (1978), 19-20.

132. For an index to church notes relating to Suffolk dating from before 1630, see J. Blatchly, *The Topographers of Suffolk, 1561-1935* (5th edn, Ipswich, 1988), preliminary matter [p. vii].

133. It should be noted nevertheless that in 1555 or 1556 Rooke Green brought an action in Chancery (TNA (PRO), C1/1429/58) counter-pleading against Dame Margaret's action against him in Common Pleas about her dower lands, after the death of Sir Edward Green (which occurred in 1554: Morant, *History and Antiquities of the County of Essex*, ii, p. 286):. It is also worth observing both that such actions might well be collusive, and that agreement in religion does not preclude disagreement about money.

134. The churchwardens' accounts for 1593 (BL Additional MS 25344, ff. 29r-30v) show the leading townsfolk Edmund Withipoll and Robert

Barker donating £20.00 each to the rebuilding, plus another loan of £20.00 from parishioners, and a London merchant Matthew Whithand giving no less than £50.00. This more or less balanced expenditure on the chancel project of £110.4s 5d in 1593. There had been earlier extensive building works in 1574-76: ibid., ff. 16r-18r.

135. BL Additional MS 25344, f. 14r. One calls to mind Wolsey's equally ruthless demolition of most of the monastic nave of St Frideswide's Oxford for Cardinal College chapel there (now Christ Church Cathedral): a demolition which is unlikely ever to be remedied.

136. BL Additional MS 25344, f. 19r. For Rooke Green's death, Morant, *History and Antiquities of the County of Essex*, ii, p. 286.

137. A small exception is the vigorous Catholic polemic of Nicholas Sander, *De Schismate Anglicano* (1585), but that only records the destruction of Our Lady of Ipswich in a regretful nationwide list of shrines destroyed by Cromwell: N. Sander, *Rise and growth of the Anglican Schism* (London, 1877), 140.

138. Bale, *A mysterye of inyquyte*, f. 30r. Of Barton and Bocking, he says 'Doctor Bockynge lyke wyse ded wonderfull feates at Caunterberye in kent by Elyzabeth Berton to sett vp a newe pylgrimage at Court vp strete.' Bocking was an Oxford DD, but he may have been from the Suffolk family of the same name at Ashbocking, or more likely took his surname in religion from origins in the Canterbury peculiar of Bocking (Essex).

139. T. Cranmer, *Catechismus, that is to say, a shorte instruction into Christian religion for the synguler commoditie and profyte of children and yong people. Set forth by the mooste reuerende father in God Thomas Archbyshop of Canterbury, primate of all England and Metropolitane* (London, 1548, *RSTC* 5993), sig. ()4v. It is interesting that the first three shrines named in Cranmer's list correspond to those named in 1527 in the sermon of his Cambridge contemporary Thomas Bilney at Christ Church Ipswich, mentioned above.

140. *The seconde tome of homelyes of such matters as were promised and intituled in the former part of homelyes, set out by the aucthoritie of the Quenes Maiestie: and to be read in euery paryshe churche agreablye* (London, 1563, *RSTC* 13665), f. 50r.

141. Grant to Edward Forthe and Henry Bett, both of Stepney, *Calendar of Patent Rolls, Elizabeth I, VI, 1572-1575*, no. 109, p. 39. A rent of 12d in Holbrook from the Daundy chantry was part of the same extensive package of such items. The second Lord Wentworth normally lived at Stepney, so Forthe and Bett were probably his household servants.

142. SROI, C/3/10/2/1, 1 and 2, listed Allen (ed.), *Ipswich Borough Archives 1255-1835: a catalogue*, pp. 333-34.

143. On these closures, D. Palliser, 'The unions of parishes at York, 1547-1586', *Yorkshire Archaeological Journal* XLVI (1974), 87-102; on Colchester, P. Collinson, *The Religion of Protestants* (Oxford: Clarendon Press, 1982), 171n.

144. TNA (PRO), PROB 11/33 (PCC 2 Coode).

Index nominum

Ady, William — 3,8
Ager, Charles — Cover
Argentine, Richard — 56
Arthur, Prince — 12
Assheton, Edmund or Edward — 15-16,42

Bailey, John — 14-17,37-9, *passim*
Bailey, Richard — 14
Bailey, Robert — 14
Baker, John — 12
Bale, John — 26-28,55,64,65
Ballard, Margery — 29
Barker, William — 45,46
Barley, Dorothy — 29
Barton, Elizabeth — 26,51,64
Barton, William — 12
Beauchamp, Richard, Earl of Warwick — 62
Becket, Thomas — 2,17,40,53,55
Bett, Henry — 66
Bilney, Thomas — 46-49,51,52
Blanche, Princess — 10-12
Bocking, Dr Edward — 65
Bothe or Booth, Robert — 15,16,42
Bowgas, Thomas — 48,51
Brandon, Charles, Duke of Suffolk — 20
Braunch, Richard — 14
Bray, Robert — 45
Bridges, John — 13,14
Brigges, John — 14,23

Bucer, Martin — 53
Buckenham, William — 14,15
Bugges, Edward — 30

Caldwell, John — Cover
Calthorpe, Abbess Margery — 27,28
Calthorpe, Mistress — 12
Canning, Richard — 59
Capon, Dr William — 43,55
Casale, Sir Gregory — 39
Charles II, King — Cover
Chitting, Henry — 63
Christmas, Katherine — 52
Clench, John — 66
Clerk, John — 39
Cordell, Sir William — 30
Cranmer, Archbishop Thomas — 28,52,53,64,65
Crewkhorne, Dr Robert — 52,53,65
Cromwell, Thomas — 51-58, *passim*
Curson, Sir Robert Lord — 23-30, *passim*
Curson, Lady Anne — 62
Curson, Lady Margaret — 30,62-64

Darkyns, John — 48
Daundy, Edmund — Cover1,3,4,6,8,9,16,17,40,56,62,66
Daundy, Joan — 17,40
Davy, David Elisha — 32,45,59-61
Delapole, earls of Suffolk — 40,41
Dorne, John — 23
Dorset, Thomas — 52
Dowsing, William — 32

Edward III, King — 6,7,10
Elizabeth of York, Queen — 12,24
Elizabeth I, Queen — 16,29,56,65

Felgate, Robert — 3
Forest, Friar John — 53
Forthe, Edward — 66
Fox, Richard — 48
Foxe, John — 2,47,57
Frost, George — Frontis

Gadarn, Derfel — 53
Gardiner, Stephen — 43
Ghinucci, Bishop Jerome — 39
Gipps, Sir Richard — 39
Green, Sir Edward — 30,63
Green, Dame Margaret — 63,64
Green, Rooke — 30,63,64
Grindal, Edmund — 29
Grose, Francis — Cover

Halteby, John — 3,6,7,62
Henry IV, King — 8,10
Henry VIII, King — 2,14,17,20,25, 37,40,46,53,56,68
Hervey, William — 63
Howard, Sir John — 12
Howard, Duke Thomas of Norfolk — 12

Jay, Benedict — 7
Jay, Joan — 7
Jay, Peter — 7

Katherine, Queen — 24,52,53

King, Gregory — 3
Kirby, John — 59
Kyrkeham, William — 8

Lambert, John — 53
Lark, Joan — 41
Latimer, Bishop Hugh — 11,24,54
Laweman, Elias — 3,7,8
Lawrence, William — 51,54-57,60
Leew, Sayeena — 5,11
Le Kurch, John — 7,8
Lee, Edward — 43
Leo X, Pope — 40
Louis, Prince — 10
Luther, Martin — 46

Marmion, Sir John — 62
Marshall, Dr Cuthbert — 42
Marshall, William — 52
Master, John — 23
Mellamphy, Robert — 1,2
Meye, Katherine — 66
Milner, Richard — 12
More, Sir Thomas — 23,27,28,48,49
Mundy, John — 3,6
Mynot, William — 13

Nottingham, William — 56

Ogilby, John — 3,4,6,8,62

Paston, John — 12
Paston, Margery — 12

Pococke, Edward Charles 67
Pykas, John 47
Pypho, John 45

Raylond, Henry 48
Reve, *alias* Melford, Abbot John 20,24,49,53
Rex, Richard 27
Rideout, John 3,8
Rideout, William 3,8
Rowe, George 5
Rush, Sir Thomas 51,52,54

Sabyn, William 56
Saye, William 13
Shaa, Edmund 30
Singleton, Anketell Cover
Smarte, Alice 49,50
Smarte, William 49,50
Smith, John 23

Tay, Thomas 71
Thacker, Thomas 54
Tunstall, Bishop Cuthbert 47
Tyllotson, William 63
Tyndale, William 23,26,46,49
Tyrrell, Anne 29
Tyrrell, Mary 29
Tyrrell, Sir Thomas 71

Ufford, earls of Suffolk 40

Veer, Henry 62
Velwet, Walter 11,12

Vere, Elizabeth de 52

Waldegrave, Sir William 30,71
Weever, John 63
Welwette, Thomas 12
Wentworth, Ann 29
Wentworth, Dame Cecily 28
Wentworth, Jane 27-29
Wentworth, John 29,63
Wentworth, Laura 30
Wentworth, Mistress 23,26,48,52,61,64,68
Wentworth, Sir Richard 71
Wentworth, Sir Roger 20,25,27,28,30,54,68
Wentworth, Sir Thomas, later Lord, 27,43,54,55
Wentworth, Sir Thomas, Second Lord, 66
Wentworth, Ursula 28,29
Westhale, Walter de 3,6
Westone, John de 6
Weybread, Richard 14
Willoughby, Sir John 71
Wingfield, Sir Anthony 24
Wingfield, Sir Humphrey 39,43
Wingfield, Sir Robert 28
Winter, Thomas 41,42
Wolsey, Joan 17,40
Wolsey, Robert 19
Wolsey, Thomas 38-43, *passim*
Woman at the almshouse, The 8
Worde, Wynkyn de 21,22
Wriothesley, Charles 54
Wriothesley, Sir Thomas 40,41

The Authors

Diarmaid MacCulloch (left) and John Blatchly (right).

Diarmaid MacCulloch

Professor of the History of the Church and Fellow of St Cross College, Oxford, was brought up in a Suffolk rectory, and his publications include much on the county; his first joint article with John Blatchly appeared in 1977. His *History of Christianity: the first three thousand years* and the BBC TV series based on it first appeared in 2009; the book won the Cundill Prize, the world's largest prize for history, in 2010. He was knighted in the New Year's Honours List of 2012.

John Blatchly

When John Blatchly came to Suffolk in 1972 to be headmaster of Ipswich School he joined the Suffolk Institute of Archaeology and History and other bodies studying the county's past. He has been Chairman since 1993 of the Ipswich Historic Churches Trust, caring for five of the town's redundant churches and finding new uses for them. His knowledge of Ipswich churches and the long history of the borough school and Thomas Wolsey, its most famous pupil, has helped him collaborate in a study which centres on the Tudor font in the parish church only three hundred yards from his home.

Back cover: Anonymous watercolour *c.*1875 showing the western range of Edmund Daundy's almshouses built on both sides of Lady Lane before he died in 1515, on the west reusing the site of St John's Hospital, the 14th century almshouse for the poor of the parish of St Matthew. The Tudor dwellings were demolished in 1877 and replaced from the estate of Joseph Hill, wireworker of the parish who died intestate but his intentions were known. Might the woman in the picture be wearing almshouse uniform? The shop with the lamp attached to it was the greengrocery kept by Charles Ager. [Reproduced by kind permission of Colchester & Ipswich Museum Services ISMG R.1918-50]

Inside back cover: Photograph from the Cornell collection from which the last watercolour might have been drawn, so closely do their details match. [Reproduced by kind permission of the Suffolk Record Office Ref. K490/170/1]